# Not Without Incident

Reminiscences of a BSAP Trooper
of the early days in Southern Rhodesia

## William Henry 'Bunny' Rabbetts

TSL Publications

The Great War in Africa Association

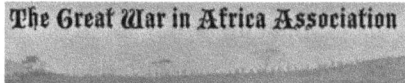

Reprinted in Great Britain in 2022

By Great War in Africa Association, TSL Publications, Rickmansworth

ISBN: 978-1-915660-07-7

First published in 2007 by the United Kingdom Branch of the British South Africa Police Regimental Association. A second edition was published 2010.

Acknowledgement and thanks go to:
*The Outpost* Magazine of the British South Africa Police
Cover Design: Alan Toms (7391)
The History Section Committee, United Kingdom Branch Regimental Association (Chairman Alan Toms)
Alan Stock (6063), Editor of *The Outpost* 1966 to 1984, who provided and edited the original typescript of Trooper Rabbetts' story.

First arranged and typeset by John Berry (5584)

Apology is made for standard of some photographs. This is caused by scanning from old magazines with poor paper quality.
The language of the day has been retained for historical accuracy.

# CONTENTS

# FOREWORD

IN MY TIME as *Outpost* Editor (1966–1984) the magazine received so many memoirs and short stories from former members of the Force that there was room to publish only a few of them. In the late Seventies the constraints on 'memoir publication' increased for two reasons: the immediacy of the war on terrorism created a gulf between the good old days and the harsh realities of policing and, by this time, the proportion of black serving members subscribing to the magazine had increased considerably so that content had to be adjusted more in their favour – and, to be honest, the African constable was rarely given much prominence in tales of the early years. Within a year or two of the BSA Police being replaced by the Zimbabwe Republic Police, the new regime flexed its muscles and the 'Old Comrades' genre, respected for nearly a century, was declared inappropriate. When Bunny Rabbetts' story arrived at the *Outpost* office is anyone's guess. Evidently written at the start of the Second World War, I can't recall meeting or even corresponding with Bunny or his family – although a contemporary of mine does remember being enthralled by his verbal reminiscences at Murray's Column reunions in the Sixties. His short story 'Wanderers', which has been included in this memoir, was published in the January 1961 Issue of *Outpost* but there is no mention of him in the Old Comrades columns of that era, nor did an obituary notice appear for him in the last twenty years of the BSAP magazine's existence.

The forerunner of *The Outpost* was *The Police Review*, first published in March 1911. Few troopers' tales of the preceding years saw the light of day and it was a long time before the new magazine became introspective enough to give space to policemen's adventures. Divertissement was the order of those days and this included the *Review's* regular publication of plays, short stories and book reviews as well as comment on the current music hall scene.

Despite Bunny's fondness for songs and minstrel shows (where his early talent as a 'cornerman' – one half of a minstrel double-act might have come to the notice of the *Review*), the only mention of Trooper Rabbetts was in 1912 after he had become a West Nicholson civilian.

This lack of individual accounts of Rhodesian police life before the First World War – quite apart from the innocence of a teenager all at sea, an adolescent trying to find his way in Cape Town and Johannesburg and a youthful soldier's baptism of fever if not of fire in the Anglo Boer War – give Bunny's *Incidents* a special place in Southern African history.

Alan Stock
Eastbourne, England
September 2007.

William Henry 'Bunny' Rabbetts joined the British South Africa Police as a Trooper in 1902, Regimental Number 374. He left in 1904, contract expired, and then re-joined in 1906, Regimental Number 819. He left finally in 1911.

MAP OF
SOUTHERN RHODESIA
Reproduced by permission
of the
BRITISH SOUTH AFRICA COMPANY

# CHAPTER ONE

## The Good Ship *Ohio*

'All Ashore..........................................................................Going Ashore!'
'All Ashore............................................................Going Ashore!'
................................................ followed by a short whistle.

On hearing these shouted directions and feeling the SS *St Louis* beginning to move, I poked my head over the rail and watched the crowd waving their farewells from the quay. The passengers were leaving friends and relatives to cross the vast Atlantic, bound for that wonderful city of New York, where some – like myself, no doubt – were full of hope of making a fortune. This was 1895 and I was not yet thirteen years old. But, after reading such boys' papers as the *Union Jack, Pluck, Sexton Blake* and *Deadwood Dick,* I'd decided that it was time for some adventure of my own and had made up my mind to run away from home. And so I found myself signed on as a bellboy on the steamship *Saint Louis.*

The second day was far from pleasant. I remember being very seasick and if one of the crew passed me while I happened to be feeding the fishes, he made things worse by repeating the old adage: 'A little fat pork on a piece of string...etc., etc.' That night in the 'Glory Hole' – where all the stewards slept – I felt very homesick as well as seasick. I thought of my mother and how, when she was cross with me, she would sing; 'Oh, where is my wandering boy tonight?'

After a couple of more days at sea, I was feeling fit and was put on to answering the bells with which the passengers summoned a steward to their cabins. I seemed to be getting on very well with my job, so much so that one of the bellboys threatened to knock my block off if I answered one of his bells again! What had happened was this: one of his bells had rung and, as he had not been there to respond at that moment, I had answered it.

I have forgotten what the young lady asked me to do but, after I had carried out her order, she gave me a couple of dimes and this got the other boy's goat. I threatened to tear off all the pretty buttons from his tunic and so we started to scrap. We were pulled apart by one of the stewardesses who threatened to report us to the chief steward. For honour to be satisfied, we vowed to fight to the bitter end when we arrived in New York.

We made landfall on the seventh or eighth day after leaving South-ampton. When all the passengers had gone ashore, I went into one of the cabins to count my tips. 'You're a budding Rothschild,' I congratulated myself as I counted the coins. I had visions of a few more trips like this one and then buying shares in the shipping company.

The next day I reminded my rival, the other bellboy, about our date to finish the fight we had started. With two other boys we went into the baggage shed on the quay, got into the elevator and went up to the next floor. We started clawing, kicking and pulling each other's hair. I finished up by pulling his tunic to pieces as promised. Then he started crying and threatened to report me to my mother and father when he got home. (I met this boy some years later in Durban and we laughed over our trip together as feuding bellboys. He had not told my parents and, as we had no further axe to grind, we exchanged more than a few convivial drinks.)

The following day the Chief Steward sent for me and said he wanted a volunteer to join a ship called the *Ohio* that had been chartered by some millionaires. She was bound for Russia, Denmark, Norway and Sweden, and then on to Spitsbergen where the tourists were to view an eclipse of the sun that I think only took place every eighty-odd years at that latitude. The job offered was what is known in nautical terms as the 'Captain's Tiger'. It meant attending to his cabin as well as taking him coffee on the bridge when he was on duty. I accepted the job, packed my sea bag and went ashore to stay at the Seamen's Rest House where I had to remain for two or three days until the *Ohio* arrived and docked. Whilst there, I met a youth who offered to show me the sights of Broadway and Chinatown. He warned me that it was dangerous for young lads to go to Chinatown unless armed. He suggested buying a couple of revolvers and said he knew of a place where we could buy second-hand guns and ammunition cheap. Off we went and bought two pinfires for a few dollars. They were the original

'Saturday Night Specials', very cheap and nasty, but weapons we presumed worked and would offer us some protection.

Off we went that evening. My companion seemed to know his way about and I followed him like a lamb  but, remembering all the adventure books I had read, I kept a close grip on the revolver carried in my trousers pocket. I was all ready to defend my guide and myself should we be rough-handled. We went up and down several of the main thoroughfares and I quite enjoyed viewing the Chinese shops.  While listening to the shopkeepers as they tried to sell us something, I couldn't help noticing how inquisitive they became, wanting to know where I came from and how old I was, had I got a mother and so forth. When at last we returned to the Seamen's Rest House, I remember being rather disappointed that the tour had not quite been the adventure I had anticipated – where I could have drawn my revolver, sent my would-be kidnappers fleeing and dealt with any other threat. Years later I thanked my lucky stars that nothing had in fact happened. Pinfire revolvers were notoriously unreliable and we could easily have ended up not just being kidnapped but shot by our own hands!

A day or so later, the *Ohio* steamed in and, as I stood on the quay watching her dock, I thought what an ugly old barge she was compared to the luxury liner, the *St Louis*. I reported to the Captain and handed my papers to him. He scowled and told me to report back to him later. After getting fixed up with a bunk in the Glory Hole, the Saloon Steward showed me the Captain's cabin, and instructed me as to my duties.

The passengers came aboard the following day. Within a few hours we had cast off and were being towed out to sea by a couple of tugs. Our voyage had started. After we'd passed the Statue of Liberty, I thought it time to make myself busy. I went to the Captain's cabin, he being on the bridge at that time of course, and made things ship-shape. Then I wandered round and noticed a girl, about my age, and a boy who was perhaps two or three years younger than the girl. They were watching the shore receding and appeared to be very excited. Spotting me close at hand, they asked me what I did on the ship. I told them I was the Captain's Tiger. 'The Captain's what?' they asked. I explained what it meant. Then they wanted to know where I came from, what my name was and so on. Their father arrived on the scene and before I was able to move off, he joined in the conversation. Then the Saloon Steward summoned me. I was informed in no uncertain terms that I was not to talk to the passengers.

With the Captain on the bridge the next morning, I started to tidy up his cabin. Whilst cleaning the washbasin, I noticed a glass of water on the side and picking it up, I went outside and emptied the glass overboard. I went back, washed the glass and replaced it on the shelf. A little later on the Captain rang for me and, on presenting myself, I was greeted with 'What the hell have you done with my teeth?' Never having seen or heard of false teeth, I had no idea what he meant. Very respectfully, I enquired what he meant. 'You bloody young fool!' he shouted. 'I left my teeth in a glass of water there,' pointing to the washbasin where the glass had stood. I confessed that I had emptied the glass overboard. 'What?' he shouted. 'You so-and-so, get the hell out of here!' and, with the help of his boot, I was sent on my way, literally 'scuppered'.

Picking myself up and properly scared, I ran as fast as I could to find sanctuary in the Glory Hole. The Saloon Steward appeared shortly after and, not surprisingly, told me that I was no longer the Captain's Tiger. My new job was to look after the boy and girl – those to whom I'd been talking when they had their meals at a special table in the saloon. This bucked me up a lot. Just before the bell rang for lunch, I was at the table I'd prepared with the help of another steward. The Saloon Steward showed the youngsters to their seats, the parents following to make sure their offspring were being properly fixed up. They were told I'd been detailed to look after them on the voyage. I remember there was ice cream on the menu that day. My charges told me they loved ice cream. After they had eaten two each, they asked me if I couldn't get some more. 'Of course,' I said, little knowing the trouble and manoeuvring I would have to go through before I managed to scrounge another four helpings from the galley. I served them one more ice cream each. The remaining two I hid in the sideboard from where we would get them later when no one was in the saloon.

On the poop deck that afternoon, the youngsters found me and asked my Christian name. Assuming that the restriction on conversation with the passengers no longer applied, I told them it was Willie. That didn't impress them. They were going to call me 'Fairy' and from then on, much to my disgust, I was known as Fairy to just about every one of the seventy or eighty passengers, all of them very rich.

In the evenings when things were quiet, a few of the crew used to gather on the deck to sing, accompanied by a banjo or accordion. Since I was supposed to have a fairly good voice, I was persuaded to sing such songs as 'My Bonny Lies Over the Ocean', 'Genevieve', 'My Old Kentucky Home' and others. The passengers sat around enjoying the performances with the little girl always in the front row. Need I mention that by this time I had fallen deeply in love with her?

It was my thirteenth birthday on the 5th of August and I received quite a few cash presents from some of the passengers, including of course my little girlfriend and her parents. A few days later the ship stopped at Southampton for a few hours but I didn't want to visit my parents in case my seafaring was abruptly brought to an end.

We continued on to St Petersburg, then the capital of Russia. Our passengers would be going on by train to Moscow and would be away several days. My heartthrob's father asked the Captain's permission to take me along with the family but this was refused. To make up for my disappointment, the father gave me several dollars and asked the Captain that if I were to be allowed ashore, would he make sure I was accompanied. He reckoned it would be wrong for me to go wandering round the city on my own. The Captain agreed to the father's request, the false teeth apparently being a thing of the past – in another sense! I felt very sad when my little girl said goodbye, but she promised to tell me all about Moscow when she came back. She would also bring me a present. This she did and, if I remember rightly, it was a fine tiepin.

I was allowed ashore in the company of one of the crew the day the passengers left for Moscow. I shall not describe where I was taken and what I saw but my young eyes were opened and I never went ashore again while in St Petersburg. When our passengers returned from their trip to Moscow, we up-anchored and steamed – I think – for Helsingsfors, now known as Helsinki. Remaining there a couple of days, we sailed on to Stockholm, then Copenhagen, then up through Norway's fiords, calling at Bergen, Tromso, Harmnerfest and others – as I remember – staying at each port for a day or so.

Arriving at the North Cape, we dropped anchor and I was allowed to go ashore with 'my people', as I called the family of my little girl. After climbing some way up the mountain, I remember there was a seat for the climbers to take a rest with a flagstaff close by. I was instructed to climb up the pole and attach a very small Stars and Stripes. Having flown the flag, we left the North Cape and went on to Spitsbergen. The eclipse took place around three in the morning, before which it was as bright as a summer's day. Many of the spectators had equipped themselves with dark glasses to witness the event while my sweetheart had found a piece of smoked glass for me. What a sight! I can't remember how long it took for the total eclipse, but it was pitch black when the sun was fully obscured and then, very gradually, it was bright sunshine again.

Leaving Spitsbergen, we set out on our homeward journey, calling at several ports on the way back through the fiords. At one place where we stopped, some of the passengers went ashore for a sleigh ride, my little girl's mother being one of them. Late in the afternoon the steam launch came from the shore and the people on board seemed to be very excited. As the launch came alongside, I overheard talk of there having been an accident. The doctor was summoned at once. Away he went to return after some time with his patients, my girlfriend's mother who had broken both her arms and another lady with one arm broken. What had happened was that the horses pulling the sleigh had bolted, the sleigh had crashed and its passengers had been thrown out.

The accident certainly cast a gloom over the ship and I was very sorry. I was allowed to go in and see the invalids every day. In the evenings the two youngsters came on deck and talked to me of their home in Virginia, their horses and the happy times they enjoyed there. They invited me to go back with them and I replied I would love to. Shortly after this, the father asked me the same question and I gave him the same answer.

We were now into the North Sea with the weather getting very rough and the seas running high. It got so bad that lifelines were run along the companionway to the forecastle and to the Glory Hole to enable the men to get to their quarters. The crew did nothing to still my fears and I well recall one remark: 'The bloody bottom will fall out of this old tub before we clear this weather!' One man suggested singing and we burst forth with that beautiful hymn 'For Those in Peril on the Sea'. Whether it was the enthusiasm we put into our singing or a simple answer to prayer that restored our spirits but we pulled through the storm safely. When we entered the English Channel, the sea was quite calm.

We arrived at Southampton the following day and, as my girlfriend was going up to London with her father and brother (the mother could not go because of her accident), I asked permission to go ashore and see my parents. This was granted. Off I went, taking with me the bearskin I had bought in Norway. When I arrived home my parents were very pleased to see me, but reckoned I was not looking well. I then told my mother that I had been asked if I would like to go to Virginia and that I had accepted. That settled it. Mother went off the deep end. 'So this is what you think of us after all the love we have given you. You are not going to America. I shall see the Captain and tell him how you ran away from your home and went to sea without our consent.'

The next day I saw my mother boarding the ship. She had her interview with the Captain, I was sent for, told by the Captain that he was sorry but I was to be discharged before the ship left for New York the following day.

That evening my other 'family' returned from London and I went straight to the father and told him what my mother had done. He was very sorry and when he told his children, my sweetheart cried bitterly. I swore that when I was older I would get to Virginia by hook or by crook. A little later the girl's mother sent for me, gave me some motherly advice and also a nice book that had been bought for me in London by the father. In this she wrote their addresses and made me promise that if ever I was in trouble and wanted help, I was to let them know at once. I lent the book to someone subsequently and never saw it again. I was given several pounds by the father and, in all the years that have passed since then, I have not forgotten these kind friends. Just before the ship sailed, I was helped ashore with my sea chest and bag and stood on the quay feeling very miserable at having said farewell to my shipmates and passengers. As the ship steamed out, the people were all on deck shouting 'Goodbye, Fairy'. My girlfriend was crying her eyes out and I was also weeping bitterly. I hailed a cab to take me home with my luggage. For days I would hardly speak to anyone.

Eventually my parents decided to send me to an uncle who was farming in Dorset, thinking it would cure me of my desire for adventure. I never saw my American friends again but years after I met a man in Cape Town who had been on the *Ohio* with me. He told me that my 'family' had visited England aboard another ship on which he was a steward and that they had recalled the *Ohio* voyage. They had asked him where I was, but all he knew was that I had gone to Africa. I heard years ago that I had been advertised for in one of the newspapers but I failed to get more information.

# CHAPTER TWO

## Johannesburg – 1897-1899

Africa called in 1897 and I made up my mind to get there by hook or by crook. With the help of friends among Southampton's seafarers who sympathized with my intention of jumping ship in Cape Town, I connived to get signed on the Union Steamship Company's *Norman*. This was a year or two before Union merged with Castle Steamships for the famous Union Castle Line but regular and reliable voyages had already been established between Southampton and Cape Town.

I was given all kinds of jobs during the voyage out. There was accommodation for some hundred-and-fifty passengers in First Class, a hundred in Second and another hundred in Third. Nearly every night concerts were held by the Third Class passengers, the majority of whom were miners and their families from the north of England. I made friends with quite a few, one family in particular by the name of Wright who were going to Elandsfontein.

To encourage immigration in those days, a party of ten 'professionals' – miners, for instance – could group themselves together to earn a reduction on their South African rail fares. It was agreed that I should be 'adopted' by one party of miners to whom I conveyed in confidence that I would be leaving the ship at Cape Town and would be making for Johannesburg. They were out to help me in any way possible.

On our arrival at Cape Town, I got ashore as quickly as I could while one of the Wrights took care of the box containing all my possessions. After they had passed through Customs, I was to meet them at the railway booking office on the quay. This I did and fell in with my party of ten. As the seats were booked, each person had to show himself at the pigeonhole of the ticket office. When it came to my turn, the clerk looked at me and shouted: 'You're not a miner.' The elderly leader of my party retorted: 'What the hell are you talking about? He's been in coal mining since he was nine years old.' A ticket was duly sold to the 'veteran' fourteen-year miner! We arranged to meet at the

Adderley Street railway station at about six that evening but knowing that my brother-in-law had a brother in town, I decided to look him up. I also wanted to send a telegram to a boyhood friend in Johannesburg who was working for a newspaper, *The Transvaal Critic*. This friend had deserted his ship some months previously.

When I found my relative-by-marriage, he did his utmost to persuade me to abandon the idea of going to Johannesburg. But I was determined. He relented to the extent of being at the station with a basket of food to help me on my way.

In those days it was a bit complicated to get a meal at any of the stations on route. One had to pay the train conductor of the train in advance and then, arriving at the station, one made a beeline for the dining room. Those who were lucky got some soup, and sometimes even managed to get a helping of the next course. Then the damned bell would go and everyone had to leave to go out and board his train, soup or no soup, or be left behind. It was small wonder that the dining rooms made so much money.

At Germiston (then Elandsfontein), the Wright family invited me to stay with them until I found a job. I thanked them but told them that I was going on to Johannesburg where I expected to be met by a boyhood friend. I wished them goodbye and, not long after, arrived at Park Station. What a difference in the size of that station today! I saw my friend on the platform and told him all the home news, his parents being in Southampton not far from mine. We loaded my luggage on to a native-driven cart and set off for Fordsburg where he was living with a Dutch family. What a hovel! Sickness and disease such as diphtheria were rampant. We decided that we would get an oil stove and cook our own food at night in order to save money, a start towards the fortune we were completely convinced we were going to make.

With the help of the editor of The *Transvaal Critic*, I got a job at two pounds per week in a fancy goods and stationery shop in President Street. My pal and I used to take our lunch with us and, on the way home at night, we would buy some meat or sausages and cook our dinner at home in the bedroom. We resolved to buy a cigarette-making machine and make some extra money by rolling and selling cigarettes – but we smoked all the profit, if there was any to start with. My pal introduced me to the secretary of the old Salisbury Mine. A religious man, he used to go to the workers' compound two or three times a week to hold church services. I was bitten by the bug and went with him, helping him to carry his folding organ. I remember one of his favourite hymns was 'Hold the Fort for I am Coming'. This he used to sing in the vernacular with all the natives joining in. Very soon I could sing some of the lines and even thought I might become a missionary. I changed my mind when I understood the natives better.

*The Critic* used to award what it called '*The Critic* Cake' to any person who was judged to have done something outstanding during the month. About this time, Barney Barnato fell overboard from the liner *Scot* as she was nearing Madeira. The Fourth Officer, I think his name was Clifford, dived in after him. He rescued the millionaire all right but Barney was dead by the time the lifeboat picked them up. However, '*The Critic* Cake' was awarded to Clifford for his gallant attempt but, as he was far away, the editor decided that the confectionery should end up with the newspaper's office boy, my pal. How proud we were when we carried off this prize. On the top of the cake was a ship made from icing sugar with the figure of a man diving overboard. We treasured the decoration for a while, but the cake was quickly disposed of.

After a few months we moved into Johannesburg where, for a change, we had meals in a cafe. I left my job and started with *The Critic*, addressing folders and sticking on stamps. I didn't stay there long.

One weekend we went to Krugersdorp to visit a friend who was in the Criminal Investigation Department. This man had been very good to my pal and told me he could get us both jobs as learners in the mill of one of the big mines near by. What we would have to do to start with was to keep a sharp eye on the mill workers as amalgam was regularly being stolen from the plates. If we succeeded in getting information leading to the arrest of the thieves, the mine company would reward us appreciably. We were taken to the mine and interviewed by the manager. He offered us a very small retainer – rewards only came with results apparently. This didn't suit my pal. It would mean giving up his job with *The Critic* where he was earning a fairly good salary. Returning to Johannesburg, I started looking around for another job. A man named Hall ran an employment office in the market buildings. I went to see him and he offered me a job as barman in the Jumpers Deep Hotel – after I had paid him the one-pound 'registration' fee. As I was short of cash, I sold my precious silver watch and chain Mother had given me and paid him the pound.

I took the next train to Jumpers Deep and presented myself to the hotel proprietor's wife. She told me there had to be some mistake as her husband had advertised for a barmaid! In fact, he had just gone to Johannesburg to fetch her. I felt very upset but the lady took pity on me. She told me not to worry as her husband would be back on the next train and would ensure that my journey was not entirely in vain. When her husband arrived with the barmaid, his wife told him my story. He was very kind, gave me a pound, and paid my fare back. He did not know the man Hall and reckoned he was a swindler who should be reported to the police. By the time I got back to Johannesburg, I was feeling very sick and I was laid up with fever for about a week afterwards.

In the meantime my pal had let *The Critic* know all about how I had been swindled. A reporter was sent to interview Hall but he'd shut up shop and vanished. That didn't stop *The Critic* carrying an article about an English lad's unfortunate experience, how he had sold his watch and chain to pay for a job and had been defrauded by a shark named Hall. A telegram was sent to my relative-by-marriage in Cape Town and he promptly wired back the fare for me to join him. There was no hint from him of 'I told you not to go to Johannesburg!' I should also mention that I was presented with *'The Critic* Cake' as a farewell gift.

The young man who shared my compartment on the journey back to the Cape was very good to me, realizing that I was still weak after the bout of fever. He saw that I got food whenever we stopped at a station. Before we arrived at our destination he told me he was going to Tasmania to be a fruit farmer.

If I cared to go along with him, he'd pay my fare and I could pay it back later. I often regret that I refused his offer. On arrival in Cape Town I went to stay with my benefactor and remained with him for several months at the old Bodega Hotel. Unwisely, I then decided to return to Johannesburg where I stayed with my pal. Things were not looking too good at this time. There were strong rumours of war. I went to Reitfontein and stayed with a mining contractor whom I'd met in Cape Town and who had promised to give me a start as learner on the rock drills. I shall never forget the first time I went down the mine with him. He showed me different parts of the mine where drills were at work on the different rock faces. The noise made by them was terrific. Together we ascended to the second level (two hundred feet, I think it was) where he stopped the cage and got out. I then had to climb the ladder all the way to the surface. I got the wind up well and truly and was very pleased when I finally reached the surface.

Shortly after this, war was officially declared so I packed my bags and made for Cape Town. First stop was Germiston Station where, after paying for a Second Class ticket, I was put into a coal truck with women and children who were also fleeing from the impending hostilities. While we were waiting there in the station, trainloads of excited young Dutchmen passed through. On seeing us refugees, they fired their rifles into the air, calling us Rooineks. Their insults continued until we reached Norval's Pont where we were fortunate enough to secure carriages to Cape Town. They were nowhere near as luxurious as the present day South African carriages – food on the journey was again a matter of pure chance – but, by comparison with the coal trucks with which the South African Republic had first sped its unwelcome guests on their way, the coaches were a luxury.

At Cape Town I found that local recruiting for the British forces had not yet started, so I decided to return home once more and try my luck there. In this my seafaring knowledge came in useful for I was able to work my passage in the old Union Company's steamship *Goth* (not to be confused with the *Gothland*) which carried me home to Southampton.

# CHAPTER THREE

## The Boer War – Briefly – 1900

In England I found that recruiting for the war was in a chaotic state. After looking round for an opportunity to join up, I decided that my best chance was back in the land from which I had come. I joined the crew of Cunard's SS *Cephalonia*, chartered by the Admiralty in the autumn of 1899, to carry troops to the Cape. On reaching port, I felt little compunction in deserting yet another ship for so worthy a cause as the 'Empire' and, going to Rosebank Camp, I joined up with French's Scouts.

With this unit, part of Lord Roberts' grand army, I took part in the initial advance on Pretoria before contracting enteric (typhoid fever) and dysentery like so many of my comrades. With other sick and wounded, I was taken by ox-wagon to Kroonstad where we were housed in the old church that had been converted into a hospital.

Arrangements were very primitive, with patients laying on the floor, attended only by Royal Army Medical Corps orderlies – and very few of these. The mortality rate was extremely high with men dying almost hourly,

I was fortunate to be soon transferred to Bloemfontein where I was received into the Military Hospital – formerly a theatre. The conversion had been very hasty and I remember that the stage was still set for Gilbert and Sullivan's well-known HMS *Pinafore*. At this hospital we were lucky to be tended by very capable and kind Australian nurses.

Some of the patients were convalescent, among them my fellow typhoid fever sufferers. Our digestive systems were not up to handling anything other than the lightest of diets – which did nothing for our very real hunger. One man in the next bed, separated from me by a small table on which the nursing staff cut up our bread and butter, evidently found the pangs of hunger, caused by his light diet, more than he could resist. Awaiting his opportunity when the nurse was temporarily absent, he raided the table and wolfed all the food he could lay hands on. Sad to relate, he died a few hours later in great agony. This incident greatly upset the enteric ward and made us bear with patience the irksome but essential light diet. With the careful attention of the nurses, I made slow but satisfactory progress and in due course was fit to be moved to Cape Town.

At the Bloemfontein Military Hospital was Dr Arthur Conan Doyle, the creator of Sherlock Holmes and other famous literary characters, who was later knighted. On our departure by train for the Cape, Dr Conan Doyle provided us with cigarettes and matches that we greatly appreciated.

In Cape Town I found myself once again at Rosebank Camp, by then been converted into a reception depot for convalescents. After further medical examinations, my repatriation to England was decreed and, for a change, I would not have to work my passage. When the hospital ship arrived at Southampton, I was sent to Port Brockhurst near Portsmouth. It was very annoying being so near and yet so far from my home and family. At first it looked as though military protocol would keep me from them completely but my mother intervened once again, had an interview with the medical officer in charge and somehow convinced him that she was best fitted to nurse me. I was allowed to go home and Mother made good her claim. I made a rapid recovery.

Thinking it was time I drew some pay, I decided to go to Christchurch Barracks, a few miles from Bournemouth. Passing through the main gates, I was astonished to get a smart 'Present Arms' from the duty sentry. I think my unusual headdress, slouch hat adorned with a bunch of feathers, had given him the idea that I was a novel brand of colonel or very senior Brass Hat. With little delay I found myself in front of the Commanding Officer who received me very cordially. For a while we talked about the war and my experiences. When I voiced my wish to draw some pay, he at once sent a telegram to Shorncliff Camp, explaining my position to the authorities there. The next day I received a cheque for a nice sum (£15, I think). Only two or three days later, yet another cheque arrived for me, a most welcome surprise! In due course I received orders to report in person to Shorncliff Camp where I met men from other 'irregular' Colonial contingents. I teamed up with a trooper from Strathcona's Horse, a fine upstanding Canadian all of six feet and three inches named Lateramour.

Shortly after my arrival, a pay corporal sidled up to us and whispered: 'Do you fellows want any cash?'

'I guess so,' drawled my pal in his broad Canadian twang.

'How much do you want?' asked the shyster.

My pal replied: 'Whaal, how about £10 each?'

The corporal said he would get it for us, stipulating that he must get ten per cent of the amount. He further explained that we had to sign an official receipt and we agreed to this. Within an hour, he was back with our cash. He must have done very well at the expense of the naïve 'Colonials' I had joined! Colonials we might have been but we were rapidly getting rich!

On the strength of our prosperity, we went up to London but after only a few days we were recalled to Shorncliff to receive 'The Royal Command'. We had been selected to be members of a Boer War contingent that was to parade at Windsor Castle on November 12th when we would be granted an audience with Her Gracious Majesty, Queen Victoria.

Before going to Windsor, the whole group of servicemen was taken to Cambridge for a couple of days where the inhabitants and university students gave us a magnificent time. A man named Bailey and I were billeted with Professor George Darwin, son of the even more famous and controversial Professor Charles Darwin. We were guests at a banquet in the Town Hall and taken around the colleges. In the evening we were entertained at a concert at, I think, the Conservative Club where Prince Ranjitsinhji, the noted cricketer, chaired the proceedings. Afterwards our genial and attentive host drove us to his home in his own coach and horses. The following morning, as Professor Darwin had an engagement in London, we were entertained by his wife and daughter and then taken to Christ Church where a service was held. On leaving Cambridge, we all marched behind two bands and between hundreds of cheering undergraduates to the station to entrain for Oxford.

The good people of Oxford seemed determined to improve on the Cambridge reception and their hospitality was greatly appreciated. The following day we left for Windsor to be met by a military band and marched to barracks where we smartened up our appearance before going on to Windsor Castle itself. We were shown parts of the historic residence not usually seen by the public. As the time approached for our audience with the Queen, we were lined up and told how to reply if Her Majesty spoke to any of us. We were in single file with men from the same regiment being kept together. I was next to another of the 'Colonial Contingent', a member of the Ceylon Mounted Infantry. The audience took place in St George's Hall. The Queen was accompanied by several members of her family, some of whom were small children and I think that the late King George VI and Princess Mary were among them.

A High Officer of the Court came out to us and intoned: 'Her Majesty awaits'. I cannot do justice to my feelings of awe when I looked upon that venerable and beloved lady as she sat surrounded by her gorgeously uniformed Indian attendants. On her left a High Court official stood holding a list of the names and regiments of the men standing before her.

He spoke as follows:

'Your Gracious Majesty, these men are from South Africa whence they have been invalided to this country. Some have been wounded, others sick with enteric and other fevers. They are members of Colonial Regiments, from Canada, Africa, Australia, New Zealand and other Colonies.'

The dear old lady inclined her head in greeting. Then the men on the left were marched up to the Queen until they were directly facing her. The Officer intoned:

'Your Majesty, these men belong to such and such a Regiment. Trooper … was wounded at …' The Queen bowed and asked the person mentioned how he was progressing. At the conclusion, the Queen addressed us collectively, hoped that we would soon be well and that we would return to our homes with pleasant memories of our stay in England.

After this our officer called for three cheers for Her Gracious Majesty, Queen Victoria. Hats came off and the cheers resounded in that ancient hall. Without warning a man on the right (it was my Canadian pal, Lateramour) yelled in his Canadian twang: '… and three colonial cheers' and there ensued a pandemonium of sound with each soldier voicing his colony's own 'war cry'. The little Prince and Princess jumped and clung to their attendants and tears came to the old Lady's eyes at this spontaneous demonstration. As we marched out, I could not take my eyes off Her Majesty. Later we were entertained to lunch by the people of Windsor. Telegrams arrived from all the London Music Halls and theatres inviting us to their shows on our arrival that evening. I often wonder what became of those who shared with me the honour of that wonderful experience in November 1900.

And then it was time to return to Africa. At Southampton we boarded the hospital ship *Oceana*. My parents whom I was never to see again were there to say goodbye.

# CHAPTER FOUR

## Anglo-Boer War – 1901-1902

We celebrated Christmas at sea and arrived in Cape Town just before the end of the year. After a few days at Mowbray Camp, I was ordered to rejoin my regiment at Johannesburg. I found them camped at the back of the old Johannesburg Hospital. My officers – among them the late Major Bettleheim, who was one of the Reform Committee during the Jameson Raid, and that wonderful man, the late Major J.J. O'Sullevan who served with the Northern Rhodesia Police in the Great War and won the DSO at Saisi near the German East Africa border – were pleased to see me. After I had given them details of my wonderful trip, O'Sullevan guessed I needed some money. Not at all bashful by then, I answered that of course I did.

'You had better go down to the Paymaster,' he said, 'and when you get your cheque, just make sure you look after it.' I thought this was the usual sound advice but, as I was expecting only a few pounds, I thought no more about it. I reported to the Paymaster's Office and asked for my cheque. The Paymaster opened the ledger, telling me that I had a nice few pounds to come. When he told me the actual amount, I almost fell on my back. Like a fool I argued with him and told him that I had drawn a lot of money in England. 'What!' he said, 'I've no information on what you've drawn. If that's indeed the case, you'll get no money from me until I hear from England.' I went back to camp feeling very down in the dumps and kicking myself for my honesty. The naïve Colonial Boy's dreams of getting rich were fading!

Orders came within a few days for the Corps to move off to Springs, from where the big drive to the north-east was to commence. If I remember rightly, we were to operate in three or four columns, our unit being attached to General French. We were chasing Christian Botha and, after passing through Bethel, we arrived at Piet Retief where we halted for a week or so. Moving on again, with a corporal named Galbraith, I was detailed to escort an officer carrying dispatches to his column operating on our left flank. A man from the officer's unit reinforced us. Before setting out, the officer instructed that should we be captured, we knew nothing about any dispatches.

Nothing exciting happened and we caught up with the other column and the dispatches were duly delivered. Corporal Galbraith and I stayed with this unit for two days, moving forward all the time. Then we received orders to return, again with dispatches carried by the same officer, to General French.

We set off very early and about midday came to a farm where, on our approach, we noticed people moving about. We closed carefully in extended order. Looking through field glasses, we saw only women. When we got to the farm, the officer asked the women if there were any men about. The answer was no. Then the women were asked if we could buy some food from them. They agreed to give us a meal. The officer thought it wise for one of us to keep a lookout from the cattle kraal. We loosened the horses' girths and I took the first sentry duty on the understanding that as soon as the others had eaten I would be relieved.

Off I went, keeping close to the wall of the kraal which lay below a small kopje. After being there about twenty minutes, I saw a man coming down the hill. He came down so far and then went back. It was very suspicious and I thought it best to get back and report. The others had just finished their meal. I explained what I'd seen and was rewarded for my pains by missing out on the food. Things did not look too good. We wasted no time in tightening our girths, mounting and moving off, all the time avoiding the kopje on our left. After going for about fifteen minutes, Corporal Galbraith complained of stomach pains and sought permission to dismount and answer the call of nature. Told to be quick, he dismounted while I held the reins of his horse. Galbraith was quietly getting down to business when all of a sudden, from the kopje, came Ping! Ping! Ping! Ping! And another Ping!

There was a mad scramble, Galbraith wasted not a moment adjusting his dress, leapt into the saddle and off we galloped after the other two. Fortunately, no one had been hit. At the time of the shots we must have been nearly a mile from the kopje but the Boers were known for their long-range shooting. After going five or six miles, we pulled up sharply when we spotted mounted men in the distance ahead of us. The officer looked through his glasses and admitted that he couldn't decide whether the riders ahead were friend or foe. The other group had also spotted us and was approaching cautiously. Galbraith suggested giving the standard recognition signal – waving a hat or helmet in a half-circle. This was done and thankfully was answered in similar manner. It transpired that the other men were advance scouts from French's column. Rejoining the main body, our officer duly reported to General French. A day or two later our mess was short of rations. I undertook to loot something in the way of provisions from the next farm we came to if a suitable opportunity arose. Then we came under fire from a large body of Boers situated on a ridge in our line of advance. We replied with a few shells dropped among the enemy before we – the scouts – were sent off to reconnoitre. Nearby was a farm, deserted except for poultry and a few pigs.

I made up my mind to get a small pig. The Scots Guards were marching along in open order nearby and, as they were passing the farm, I observed a few of them breaking ranks and sneaking into the farmyard. There they started to chase and capture fowls, turkeys and anything in this line. Meanwhile I'd managed to collar my pig and called on one of the Jocks to lend me his bayonet to finish it off. This he did and I had the pig in front of me across the saddle, riding along behind the Scots Guards when the Boers dropped a shell fairly close to us. My horse reared, off came the pig and away we went with me holding on for dear life. When I regained control and went back for my pig, it had gone – the Guards had got it.

A few days later I was out on the advanced scouting detail with O'Sullevan and about a dozen others. Breasting a rise, we saw we were approaching a plantation, close to which was a goat kraal within a stone wall. As we were passing, we were fired on from the plantation. O'Sullevan ordered us to gallop and take cover in the kraal. On my right was a Dutch Colonial whose name I have forgotten. I heard him shout: 'Ek is klaar!' meaning 'I am finished.' Looking in his direction, I saw him fall from his horse, which galloped on for only a short distance before it too was shot. O'Sullevan's horse was hit in the rump as its rider was dismounting to scramble over the wall. The rest of us were about to dismount when O'Sullevan, recognising the danger we were in, yelled for us to get back to the main column for help. I hoisted myself back into the saddle and set off, hell-bent for safety, followed by the others. Shots were hitting the ground all around but we got out of range safely and reported to the column. A strong detail cantered off to rescue O'Sullevan and the others. The plantation was shelled shortly afterwards and then the Scots Guards went through clearing up what was left.

Memory fails me as to the names of the senior officers who commanded the columns operating with us, but I do remember Smith-Dorrien, Bindon Blood and Dartnell. We eventually arrived at Vryheid where General French took up quarters. A well-remembered incident was when I was detailed to carry a dispatch – I think it was to General Dartnell. He was camped about four miles outside Vryheid. As often happened, I was given a return dispatch to take back to General French. On nearing Headquarters, I saw General French and his Staff Officer walking up and down on the sidewalk, smoking cigars. In such exalted presence, I smartly saluted General French by bringing my right hand smartly up to my forehead. Of course, being a cavalryman, this was wrong and I should have saluted with a straight downward right arm. The Staff Officer noticed it and, shortly after I had reported, O'Sullevan was sent for. I heard afterwards that General French and his aide had been highly amused at my salute but O'Sullevan gave me a stern admonition – quite rightly too!

Eventually we entrained our horses, it must have been at Newcastle, and returned to Johannesburg. After being there a few days I was offered staff duties back in Cape Town in the old main barracks. I accepted the transfer, made my way south and eventually arrived to start my new job. It was fortunate I was back in Cape Town because my younger brother arrived from the old country soon after. When he discovered my presence, he deserted his ship in the best family tradition. He had previously served in Kitchener's Horse and had been wounded at Nooitgedacht in December 1900. He'd been invalided home and discharged.

Recruiting was now underway for Scott's Railway Guards, destined to operate round Kimberley, Devondale, Salt Pan and that general vicinity. My brother and I reckoned the prospects were promising and we decided to join up together. Accordingly, I took my discharge from French's Scouts. Together with other recruits we were sent to Kimberley where we camped at the Wesselton Mine, with accommodation in the old stables. After patrolling this part of the country for a couple of months and exchanging a few shots with scouts attached to roving bands of Boers, we were moved up to Devondale where Tollie de Beer and his commando were threatening communications. From Devondale, patrols were sent out during the day but at night, those who had not been on patrol boarded a special armoured train at dusk and were taken along the line. Apart from trying to damage the line itself, particularly the culverts, the Boers were known to try and cross with their livestock.

The original tactics were that one man detrained at every eighth telegraph pole. There he had to remain until daylight when the armoured train collected the pickets. Our orders were to lie low and watch for any Boer movement. Should we see mounted men advancing, we were to fire on them. Then the men on our right and left, hearing the shots, would also shoot – thus sending the alarm down the line. The alerted armoured train would immediately move towards the intrusion, bringing its searchlights into use.

The single sentry business was so harrowing that it was quickly modified to three men at each picket, doing two hours on and four off. But it was still nerve-racking. You would be staring into the darkness when for no apparent reason a korhaan would be flushed. But instead of a bird, one would imagine a Boer or a whole commando. You'd catch a glimpse of a firefly – instantly translated into an enemy lighting his pipe!

However, one night something did happen. At about three in the morning, one of the pickets on my right fired, we followed suit and so down the line. Then we caught sight of mounted men and cattle. Within a very short while the train appeared, advancing towards us with its search light blazing. By this time the Boers knew they were barred from crossing the railway line and tried to turn their cattle and sheep back the way they'd come. The armoured train went into action with its machine guns. Later, another armoured train arrived, picked us up and took us back to Devondale. There we saddled up, swallowed a hasty mug of coffee and, with dawn breaking, returned to the scene of the engagement to set off on the trail of the Boers. I forget the extent of enemy casualties when we came upon the enemy but we captured many cattle and sheep. More livestock had been slaughtered in the early hours by the train's machine guns. We ate well for a week.

Later, while on patrol and nearing a farmhouse in extended order, two or our men were shot. One died at once, the other was carried to the station office at Salt Pan. The patrol returned to Devondale and a message was sent through to Vryburg for a doctor who arrived some time later. My brother and I were detailed to escort the doctor, unarmed, to Salt Pan. The wounded man was alive when we reached there but died shortly afterwards.

My brother and I were ordered to return to Devondale, leading the horse the doctor had ridden. Nearing Devondale, some wandering Boers fired on us. We spurred our horses and went like hell. Fortunately, the doctor's horse caused no trouble; he seemed to think we were at the racetrack and he was the bookmaker's favourite. A few of our men were captured soon after but were released as soon as they had been deprived of most of their kit. One of them was a great gambler who used to run the Crown and Anchor Board. At the time of his capture he had the dice in his pocket. The Boers found the dice and asked him how the game was played. It seems he lost not only his shirt – when he got back he was also minus his pants. He was more fed up at losing his dice, his main source of income, than anything else.

After completing six months guarding the railway one way or another, we decided to take our discharge and eventually arrived back in Cape Town. There was already talk circulating about an armistice and, shortly after, it was announced that the war was over. My brother went home but I wanted more from Africa. Hearing that a Sergeant Major Spence of the British South Africa Police was in Cape Town looking for recruits, I sought him out and, after passing a medical, found myself with five others bound for Rhodesia, the land of promise.

# CHAPTER FIVE

## BSA Police 1902-1904

One evening in July 1902 we left Cape Town and after travelling for about five days in the train, reached Bulawayo. Met at the station by a mule wagon that was to take us to the camp, we arrived at about seven in the evening and were shown into an old wood and iron barrack room. The occupants were busy cleaning their kit and we couldn't help but notice that they were even burnishing the heel plates of their rifles and boning their boots. It transpired that these men were getting ready for main guard the following morning.

I enquired what the life was like on an outstation and was advised that if I could get to Mashonaland with No. 3 Division, there was a chance of seeing some fighting. A troop had already been sent up from the Matabeleland Division (No. 2) to assist in the capture of a native chief named Mapendela who, with his followers, had been raiding into Portuguese territory before being chased back over the border near Mount Darwin into Mashonaland. But it was more likely that we would be assigned to No. 2 Division to strengthen the remaining Matabeleland contingent. I spoke to one of my companions from Cape Town and we decided that in the morning when we were taken before the Officer Commanding, Colonel Bodle, and he wanted us to remain in No. 2 Division, we would say there must have been some mistake. We had joined up for No. 3 Division. The other Cape Town recruits felt the same way. I can only remember the names of three of them: Algy Beck, Maudie Allen and Williams. Beck and Allen had served with Captain Masterman, as he was then, in the Army Service Corps.

The following morning we were duly called to the office and interviewed by Colonel Bodle. He started by saying he wanted men for the Battery. I have forgotten who was our spokesman but he replied – as we'd agreed beforehand – that in Cape Town we had joined specifically for No. 3 Division. The Colonel got very cross and told us to get out of the office. We didn't wait around for his decision. Later on, the Regimental Sergeant Major, also named Bodle and a nephew of the Colonel, told us to go to the Ordinance Store to draw boots, blankets, bully beef and other bits of equipment and then to pack our kit and be ready to leave for Gwelo by wagon. In those days the railway line between Bulawayo and Gwelo had not been completed. We packed up and trekked out of Bulawayo that afternoon.

I've forgotten how many days it took us to reach Gwelo, but we enjoyed every minute of it. On the last day a mounted trooper who'd been instructed to be on the lookout for us, met us and escorted us into the town. It was evening so we were given a decent meal before being shown to a grass shack where we slept. I think we remained there for a day and then got a lift on the construction train which was returning to Salisbury for more raw materials for the railway.

It took us a couple of days more to get to Salisbury and then a mule wagon ride to the camp repeated our Bulawayo experience. We were greeted by the well-remembered and very respected Regimental Sergeant Major Jimmy Blatherwick and the first thing he did that morning was to take us to the canteen where the person in charge was told to get us something to eat and drink. After this, an NCO took us to our grass hut, leaving us with instructions to fall in at two o'clock in front of the Orderly Room, which had been pointed out to us. There were only a few men in camp, as the rest had gone up to the border chasing Mapendela.

At two o'clock we lined up outside the Orderly Room. As soon as he stomped up the RSM started on Beck, standing on the right of the line:

'And what's your name, my man?'

'Beck, Sir.'

'And what regiment have you been in?'

'The Army Service Corps, Sir.'

'Oh! So you are one of those scoundrels who rob the troops of their rations.'

The RSM moved to the next man.

'What's your name?'

'Allen, Sir.'

'And what regiment have you served in?'

'Army Service Corps, Sir.'

'Oh! Another robber of the troops' rations.'

And so it went on, until he came to me.

'What is your name?'

'Rabbetts, Sir.'

'What? Rabbits?'

"No, Sir. Rabbetts.'

'How do you spell it?'

'R - A - two Bs - E - two Ts and an S.'

'Oh, is that so? Well, we want no horses' tails and manes here, young man. Get your hair cut.'

My first thoughts of the RSM were not the kindest but later on I learned to have the greatest respect for him. He treated all of us like a father. After this he asked us individually what we had joined the Police for. I replied that it was to carry out the laws of the country.

'You are here to prevent crime, not to make it.'

We then drew rifles and, after going through a few drill movements, were told that we would be leaving by wagon for Mount Darwin the following morning. We were very pleased to hear this, looking forward to a scrap with Mapendela and his merry men and also remembering the troopers we'd left in Bulawayo busy polishing their kit. With George Schlachter in charge of the wagons, we moved off the following morning. I can remember seeing dozens of reedbuck and ostriches as we were approaching Mount Hampden over the Gwebi River Flats and I also recall how well George kept us in meat for the whole journey.

After leaving Mazoe where we camped that first night, we heard lions on several occasions. I can't say I enjoyed the experience but years later I was to become accustomed to their nocturnal grumbling in many different parts of Southern and Northern Rhodesia.

On arrival at Mount Darwin, where there was a permanent Police Camp and the Native Commissioner's offices, we off-loaded the wagons. The late Bert Collier, who later transferred to the CID as a founder member of the

Department, was one of the troopers there where we remained for a day or two. Then we were ordered to trek off with native carriers to a place near the Portuguese border, the name of which I've forgotten. At the border we set the natives to making grass shelters and also a lookout tower where we had a man always on watch. We did duty there for about two months during which not a single exciting event took place other than the shooting of a lion by one of the NCOs.

Eventually we returned to Mount Darwin and remained there until the wagons arrived to take us back to Salisbury. The rains had started so no time was wasted before starting on the return trip. Should the rivers rise, we could be held up for ages. It rained nearly every day and it was far from pleasant trying to sleep under the wagons with the rain beating in. We were very thankful to reach Salisbury at last.

In those days an Irishman named John Johns was running the mess. It was all very primitive. You lined up outside the kitchen with your plate and took your turn at being served. If you thought that the food being dished up was insufficient or badly cooked and dared to complain to John Johns, you had to be literally on your toes – or you would be flat on your back! Johns reacted to complaints with a wallop about the head or, even more violently, subjected his critics to a vicious head-butting. The man was like a goat. But some of the men refused to be bullied and many were the scraps I watched between Johns and his customers. However, the food was not that bad and, taking him all round, Johns was not a bad fellow. The last I heard of him he was on Robben Island attending to the lepers so he must have had a caring side!

It was nearing Christmas and RSM Jimmy Blatherwick asked me to give him a hand organizing the Sergeants' Mess (Festive) Dinner. Colonel Flint and the other officers were to be present. I must have made a good impression as I was then asked to run the Sergeants' Mess. That experiment went well enough and, after a month or so, I was offered the Troops' 'Wet and Dry' Canteen to run. Then, with the amalgamation of No. 2 and No. 3 Divisions in mid-1903, Sergeant Major Hanson from Bulawayo took over the catering and management duties. To compensate for the earlier period of boredom on the border, life in Salisbury after Christmas brightened up considerably with several interesting incidents taking place. Colonel Flint took himself off to India to buy camels, having somehow convinced the Administration that they would be of great value to the country for transport work and carrying mails out to the districts. The ungainly animals arrived at the station one Sunday morning and, after being off-loaded, were to be taken to the Transport Camp. While the newcomers were being led through the streets, mules and horses attached to all sorts of wagons made for the hills! Carts were smashed and even the rickshaw boys abandoned their rickshaws and followed the horseflesh, scared to death at the sight of the strange intruders. The horses and mules only had to get one whiff of the camels and they were off.

I was having a few words with Sergeant Darkie Martin when we saw four camels being ridden into camp, Colonel Flint on one and three Indians on the others. On arrival outside the Officers' Mess, the Colonel shouted something – it sounded like 'Hackow' – and down went the camels. The Colonel went into the Officers' Mess while a crowd gathered and stood gazing at the peculiar livestock. Shortly after, the Colonel emerged with some of the other officers. One of the more daring spectators yelled 'What about a riding school, Colonel?' 'All right,' he replied, 'Get on, two at a time.' With this, some of the men got mounted. The Colonel shouted to the camels and they promptly got up – hindfirst! It was so sudden and unexpected that half the men fell off, over the camels' necks. With roars of laughter from the spectators, that ended the riding school.

Previous to this, Colonel Flint had established the tradition of making every Wednesday afternoon a half-holiday and inviting the towns-people to come to the camp, listen to the band and watch any sport that might have been arranged. On one occasion we had donkey races and my job was to amuse the kids. I was dressed up as a clown and wearing a mask so the youngsters couldn't recognise me. The band played on and I tried to coax one of the donkeys into waltzing. That wasn't very successful so I mounted the donkey, back to front. Turning his tail around, I pretended to the kids that my mount was a barrel organ. But, unnoticed by me, one of the bandsmen, the cornet player, came up to the donkey and blew a top note right in its ear. Up went the donkey's head; down went yours truly! As I was getting up, the brute kicked me right at the base of my spine. I went head over heels while the kids roared with laughter, at the same time trying to pull off my mask. Dr Fleming, who happened to be at the show, came across and enquired if I was all right. When I told him where I'd been kicked, he told me to try and get to the Camp Hospital. There he examined me and concluded that I had damaged my coccyx. At times I still feel the pain there, a reminder of those many years ago.

On another occasion, the inventive Colonel Flint arranged some tent pegging and 'Cutting Off the Turk's Head'. Several riders were involved and, after the tent pegging, went on to decapitate 'The Turk'. One NCO started off and, as he came abreast of his target Turk, slashed at it and promptly cut off his horse's right ear. Away went the horse, past the stables, to finish up somewhere near the Makabusi River.

'Stables' were in progress one morning when two troopers started a fight. They were both put under arrest and warned by Jimmy that they would be on the carpet at ten o'clock. There's little doubt that before the appointed time, Jimmy had had a quiet word with the OC. The first man was marched in, the charge was read out and the miscreant asked for an explanation. He told the Colonel that the other man had called him a bloody bastard and a few other choice epithets. He wasn't going to stand for that! The OC then asked him if he was prepared to box the other man. 'Yes, Colonel,' he replied. 'Very good,' said the Colonel. 'Mr Blatherwick, see that the ring is fixed up on the Square at two o'clock. We'll have this matter settled in short order. 'Very good, Sir.' 'March him out and bring in the next prisoner.'

The same questions were put to the other ruffian and he also agreed to fight. At two o'clock the ring was set up using horse lines. All the extras were laid on – buckets of water, towels, sponges and so on – but no gloves! Everyone in camp assembled and what a fight followed! Only when there was blood streaming in abundance from both men's faces did Colonel Flint decide they'd had enough. He congratulated the trooper he had declared the winner saying, 'Damned good, man! Damned good! Make him a corporal, Sergeant Major!' Two weeks later the victor was a corporal.

One night a week the band played outside the Officers' Mess but also provided some entertainment for the rest of us. We would wrap our mosquito nets around us and, thus 'dressed', become female partners for the old fashioned waltzes.

We also had our minstrel troupe. I was one corner man and 'Hacker' Mathews my opposite number. One Saturday night, we gave a concert at the Old Avenues Hotel in order to raise money – I think it was for the hospital. The place was packed and we made over fifty pounds. It was mentioned in the paper the following Monday that the hit of the evening was a song by one of the troupe called 'On the Banks of the Wabash Far Away.' I wonder how many are left who remember it? A decade later, it became the Indiana State Song.

After a while I was sent to open up a station beyond Mazoe at a place called Makopes, so named after a local chief. Before leaving, I was asked by band members to take their pet baboon with me. It had got loose during lunchtime and invaded Jimmy's office, tearing up papers, upsetting the ink and generally causing havoc. The RSM had ordered it out of camp or it would be shot.

My pack donkeys were loaded up with Chico the baboon perched on top of one of them, fastened with his chain. After a chorus of farewells from what seemed to be every man in camp, I set off. I had to pass the old Government House but, nearing there, I encountered one of our troopers who couldn't resist poking fun at the baboon and making rude noises directed at Chico's mount. It was enough to upset the fresh-from-the-stables donkey. It promptly bolted with the second pack donkey in hot pursuit, my dog bringing up the rear and barking like hell. The next thing I saw was the packsaddle, having been jolted loose, sliding down under the donkey's belly. Poor old Chico was being dragged along and turning involuntary somersaults. When the saddle got completely under its belly, the donkey had to stop. I caught up with him and with the help of my native constable we unchained the baboon. What a sight he presented! His eyes were swollen and I swear he was crying. But after careful examination, I seemed that only his pride was injured.

Despite his violent fall from grace, Chico obediently followed along as far as Avondale when I called him. He climbed up my leg and sat in front of me on the saddle. It was great fun seeing him and the dog playing the fool along the road. At times Chico would get on the dog's back for a few seconds before unceremoniously being heaved off.

After staying at the Mazoe Camp for the night, I moved on with my circus. The next night was spent at Jack Southey's farm. I've forgotten its name, or the river on which it was situated, but it was not far from the old Kimberley Reef Mine which years later I was to get to know well.

Eventually we arrived at Makopes where I hired labour and started to build the camp. About two weeks later a runner brought me the news that three or four men had been detailed to join me.

The first trooper arrived a few days later as I was frying some fat cookies and I gave him a couple. He took them on a plate which he put in the hut. Shortly after I heard a shot. What had happened was that Chico had seen the cookies being left in the hut, had gone in, helped himself, and made off at a run with his mouth full and another biscuit in each hand. The new arrival chased Chico up a tree before fetching his gun to shoot the baboon. When I got there, poor Chico was on the ground, quite dead, still holding the cookies and with tears streaming from dead eyes. I felt like shooting the newcomer. He was very apologetic about the incident and begged me not to let the men know in Salisbury how Chico had really met his end.

Just before leaving Salisbury to open up the new station I had been suffering from toothache and had got a requisition from the doctor to have one back tooth extracted and two front ones stopped. I went to the dentist employed by Strachan the Chemist in Manica Road and known for 'lifting his elbow' quite frequently during the day as well as at sundown. An appointment was made for me for ten o'clock the following day. I arrived at the dental surgery and found him very rather the worse for wear. He told me to get into the chair and put a gag between my teeth effectively muzzling me. He then put the gas mask over my face and started to pump. It made me feel a bit dizzy but didn't knock me out completely. Before I knew what was happening, he had the back tooth out and had then extracted the two front ones which should only have been stopped. I started to twist and turn, at the same time trying to protest at what he had done. After a great deal of struggling, he eventually removed the gag and demanded, in a very bleary voice, to know what all the fuss was about. One can imagine what my speech was like, with my front teeth missing, spitting and spluttering blood and very angry into the bargain. I managed to make him understand what he had done. He looked at the requisition and saw his mistake. He begged me not to report his negligence and promised to make me a plate, with two teeth, that would be the very best in the country. Not a soul would notice the difference from my own teeth. Of course, he wouldn't charge me for the plate. What could I do but agree?

In a couple of days I had them fitted – to stretch a point. After a week or so they jumped all over the place. But what fun I had with the raw natives by pushing the two incisors out suddenly. They would stare in amazement, unable to understand what had happened (as I'd quickly got my fangs back into position). Then I would shoot them out again and they would run as if the devil himself was in pursuit.

At the camp one morning, two native women came in to barter some eggs and tomatoes for salt. They were standing on the square when I spoke to them. I thought I'd have some fun and, as they were looking straight at me, I shot out my false fangs. Their eyes bulged as I shot my teeth in and out. That settled it. They dropped the baskets of eggs and tomatoes and ran screaming *'Maiwe, Maiwe*!' Soon all I could see were two loincloths of buckskin fluttering in the distance. The two women never came to barter again.

Not far from the camp was a trader, an ex-policeman whose name escapes me. Visiting him one day, I arrived just after he had shot a black-maned lion that had killed a native woman in the lands. The lion had sprung on the woman, killed her, and was carrying her away when other natives, who had witnessed the attack but had been powerless to intervene, sneaked back to the trader and told him what had happened. He got his gun, went after the lion and came on it as it was having its meal. He killed it on the spot. Whilst hunting klipspringer in the Granite Hills one day, with one of my police boys, I came across some rocks piled up in front of what looked like an opening into a cave. We pulled down the rocks and, on looking inside, we found about twenty muzzle-loading rifles, no doubt been hidden there by the rebels. I recruited several natives from a nearby village and made them carry the rifles back to my camp. The local chief and his men of course denied all knowledge of the arms cache. Later I had the rifles taken to Salisbury where Jimmy Blatherwick congratulated me on my discovery. The natives in that part of the country were known to still be a bit wild!

About this time, Jimmy had given orders for all staff members to attend morning riding school at the back of the Camp Hospital. On the staff as a tailor was a Scotsman, McPhearson, but called 'McBung' by the men. He came from the Isle of Skye and when he got excited nobody could understand him, his Scotch accent was so broad. Poor old McBung, I believe, had only ever ridden a Shetland pony, if that! However, he had to parade with rifle at the riding school with the rest of the 'honourable dismounted'. As they were trotting around and about, Jimmy cut at McBung's horse with his whip. Away went the tailor and his horse with Jimmy yelling after them, 'Where the hell are you going without permission, McBung?'

Horse and rider vanished into the distance. About an hour later a very angry McBung was seen leading his horse into camp shouting, 'Ma name is noo McBung. Ma name is McPhearson.' After he had off-saddled he came into the mess hut, raving and vowing to have Jimmy up before the Colonel for victimisation or something. But first he demanded to see Captain McQueen and was told to be at the office at ten o'clock. In the meantime, of course, Captain McQueen had seen Jimmy and arranged things. McBung duly appeared before Captain McQueen, still very excited and still insisting, 'Ma name is noo McBung, ma name is McPhearson.'

As part of the charade it was decided to send for Sergeant Stewart to act as official interpreter. After much palaver, Jimmy promised he would not address the tailor as McBung again. The next morning McBung paraded at morning riding school. Jimmy waited his chance and then flicked his whip on McBung's horse. The unceremonious retreat of the previous day was repeated with Jimmy shouting, 'Where the hell are you off to without permission, Mr...' – he hesitated – 'McPhearson? I didn't call you McBung that time, did I?' The poor old tailor returned to camp later but this time refrained from laying a complaint about his treatment.

I spent another month or so at Makopes before having to go to Mazoe for some reason or other. I was not feeling too well the morning I left camp and after getting only about five miles from camp my horse started to shiver and would hardly move. I decided to off-saddle and the horse promptly collapsed. I got my blankets unrolled and laid down in the shade. Within an hour my horse was dead and by this time I could hardly move, shivering and feeling icy cold. I covered myself with the blankets and somehow managed to write a note explaining my position to send back to camp with the police boy. After waiting three or four hours some boys arrived with a hastily made machila. They placed me on the stretcher and carried me back to camp – after I had instructed them to sever the off-front hoof of the horse (where the troop number had been branded) and also its tail.

During the night the fellows took turns in 'bossing me up'. I was in a pretty bad way and slightly off my rocker. Early next morning I was back on the machila and with about ten carriers and two police boys we were on our way to Mazoe where the nearest doctor was stationed. How these boys looked after me and did all they could for me! About four o'clock we arrived at Jack Southey's farm. Mrs Southey took charge at once and put me to bed. I was told later that she fully expected me to get blackwater fever as I was showing all the symptoms. What she gave me I don't know but the sweat poured out of me. I have never forgotten her kindness.

The next morning I felt a bit better and it was decided that I'd better get to Mazoe as soon as possible. Off we went again to arrive at the Mazoe Police Camp during the afternoon. Dr O'Keiff was sent for and when he'd examined me he decided to have me sent by buckboard to Salisbury Hospital. I pleaded with him not to send me there, as I'd had more than enough of hospitals and hated them. He relented and I slowly recovered.

After a while I started patrolling around the Mazoe Valley. There were only a few farms there in those days: the concession being farmed by the Southey family and the two Biggs brothers. The latter had a sister visiting them from the Old Country. While she was there, lions visited the farm and killed some cattle. It was decided to erect a platform in the branches of a big tree near where a part of a carcass had been left by the beasts. The brothers, expecting the lions to return to the kill, intended to get up on the platform with their rifles about sundown in the hope the lions would appear and they would have a chance of bagging them.

Their sister didn't want to be left at the farmhouse alone and joined the brothers on the platform. There was precious little room to spare and heaven knows what would have happened had the platform collapsed when the lions appeared – which they did during the night. If I remember correctly, the Biggs brothers killed one and wounded another. Their sister said afterwards that she would not have missed the experience for all the tea in China ... and she probably drank a great deal of it while relating her lion-hunting times in Rhodesia.

As my contract of service was drawing to a close, I decided to take my discharge and did so in August 1904. I went back to Cape Town, where I remained with my brother who had returned from home. During this time I met an old girlfriend whom I'd known when I was with French's Scouts. Reading the paper one morning, I saw an account of an accident that had taken place on Long Street. A woman had been knocked down and run over by a tram and the description given made me think it was my girlfriend. The police were appealing for someone to view the body awaiting identification at the mortuary. The account worried me all day and it was not until about seven o'clock in the evening when I decided to go to the police station in Wale Street.

It was November. It was raining hard with much lightning and thunder. At the police station I told them that I thought I could identify the body and the sergeant-in-charge detailed a constable to take me to the mortuary, situated in a gloomy back street. On the way the policeman told me how much he hated these mortuary duties. Reaching our destination, he opened the first door that led into a small courtyard. From there another door had to be unlocked which opened into one ward of the mortuary. He switched on the light and, looking around, we saw no bodies on any of the stone tables. We started forward to the next room when, all of a sudden, there was a great crash of thunder and out went the lights. 'Hell,' shouted the constable. 'I'm off.' Away he went with me close behind. Once outside, he confessed, 'I can't stand this, it gets on my bloody nerves.' I'm afraid I told him it was his job to show me the body so back we went. Just as I entered the second room, there was another crash of thunder and my escort was away again, me after him but this time to catch him and get this business over and done with. I grabbed him near the first door, just as the lights came on.

'Play the game and go in yourself,' suggested the policeman. 'I'll stand by and if the lights go out again I'll light matches so that you can see your way out.' I went back and in the second room or ward, saw the body on the table. I gingerly pulled back the shroud to look at the face but it was impossible for me to be certain that it was the person I knew although some of the clothes on the ground looked familiar. I quickly left to return to the police station with my brave escort and report my failure at identification.

A day or two later I was walking through the gardens with another lady friend and, on rounding one of the turnings, I came face to face with the girl I had gone to identify. She gave me a nasty look as we passed while I felt like falling through the earth. My companion asked me if I was ill. I replied that I was not feeling too fit and that I'd better go home as I thought I might have a touch of Rhodesian fever.

There and then I resolved never to volunteer to identify a body again during a thunderstorm, when it was possible for the lights – or lack of them – to play havoc with nerves already at high pitch and especially in the company of an escort even more apprehensive than oneself.

# CHAPTER SIX

## Johannesburg Fire Brigade – 1905

Hearing that an old friend, Bill Rowe, who had been in the Cape Town Fire Brigade, was now Second Officer in the Johannesburg Fire Brigade, I decided to return to Johannesburg with the hope of fulfilling one of my boyhood dreams: that of being a fireman, wearing a shining brass hat, rescuing fair maidens entrapped in lofty bedrooms and carrying them down fire escapes to safety and their eternal gratitude.

Arriving in Johannesburg, I went to see Bill at the fire station on the old Von Brandis Square. He informed me there was no vacancy at the moment but that he would do his best to get me in should something come up. After waiting a week or two Bill sent for me, said that there was now a vacancy and that I was to have an interview with the Chief. The interview duly took place where I was told that I would be tested and, if successful, I would be signed on.

With this the Chief got up and, followed by the Second Officer and myself went outside where he blew his whistle. Men immediately sprinted out of the engine rooms. 'Jumping sheet and scaling ladders,' ordered the Chief.

My God, I thought, what's going to happen now. Then I saw the men making for the corner building carrying the ladders and other equipment. The Second Officer – to mix metaphors – started to pull my leg about breaking my neck. 'Take no notice,' grinned the Chief. 'When I say "jump" – jump!'

When we reached the corner, the men busied themselves assembling the scaling ladders. One man climbed up, taking with him the hook ladder. He hooked it into position from the coping, leaving it swaying there from side to side. Then came my baptism of fire – without the fire. I was told to climb the scaling ladders, transfer to the hook ladder, and so up to the coping.

Then I was to stand up on the coping – which I must mention was no more than eighteen inches wide – and wait for the order to jump. When I realised what was expected of me, all thoughts of rescuing fair maidens went flop. What made it worse was the fact that passers-by, guessing what was about to take place, deviated from their course and clustered around to watch a damn fool break his neck – if I did not jump clean into the canvas sheet being held out by about a dozen midget-sized men below me. However, when I got to the coping and stood up, my knees were knocking together to such an extent that I felt even more of a fool. All the people watching me and, of course, laughing didn't help.

I waited. When the Chief shouted 'Jump', I closed my eyes and gave one leap. I would have landed on the ground; only the firemen below were practised, prepared and pulled out just in time to catch me in the sheet. After bouncing in the air two or three times, I managed to get my breath back.

The spectacle over, we all went back to the station. In the Chief's office he confirmed the success of my trial by ordeal and signed me on. I was handed over to the storekeeper who issued me with my uniform and other bits and pieces. Taking all this to my quarters, shared by about five other men, I waited my opportunity to try on my brass hat in front of the mirror. A gladiator grinned back at me. The chances of fair maidens being rescued by him improved considerably.

I was detailed to join the crew of the fire tender, the second machine summoned to any conflagration. Anticipating a call-out, I was told to put my helmet, belt and axe at the appointed place on the tender. At this stage I had no idea what kind of machine the tender was but one of the crew showed me. Some of the machines were parked on one side of the road opposite the building where our sleeping quarters were. The horses were stabled on the same side, behind the first machines to leave for the fire. It was all very well organized. As soon as the fire bells went, a lever would be pressed down in the watch room that would automatically release the bolts of the stable doors. Out would trot the well-trained horses to their appointed machine. I finished polishing my helmet and adjusting my other kit and was on my way to place them on the tender when suddenly the Gamewell fire alarm rang out the code to indicate whence the callout had come. Then the alarm bells proper started to ring. Men sprinted to their machines as I watched in amazement. One horse, a grey, obediently trotted past me and I swear gave me a look as much as to say, 'What the hell are you getting in my way for. Get a move on!' 'Come on you bloody fool, don't just stand there like a mummy.' The shout came from the tender which was just moving out of the engine room. I was grabbed by the hair and hauled up on to the machine. I was almost thrown off as we left the station and turned sharply to the right but I managed to grab the fellow who was sitting next to me around the waist. 'What the hell's your game? Do you think I'm your old woman?' More helpfully he told me to hang on to the rail that was there for the purpose. I watched him fasten on his axe-belt and wondered how I could follow suit without letting go of the rail and falling off the machine. Somehow, I managed it.

The fire was on Commissioner Street: three shops well alight and a crowd of spectators already. As we pulled up to a hydrant, the horses were unharnessed and led to safety. The rest of the crew dismounted leaving me still on the tender not knowing what to do.

'Hand out the hose,' they shouted.

'Where is it?' I asked.

'In the well,' they shouted.

One fellow got up, lifted the seat where we'd been sitting and revealed fifty and one hundred feet coils of hose. I started handing them out but while doing so, the seat fell on top of me, leaving my legs dangling outside I was rescued in time to hear a shout for the scaling ladders. Again, I didn't know where to find them until the driver showed me where they were. Off I started across the road with one length to where they were wanted. Other men brought more and they were placed in position so that a man could climb to the first floor.

Then I was told to help the driver who was running out a length of hose from a passageway. We finished up in front of a tobacconist's shop, the interior of which was well ablaze. The order was given to smash the door lock to allow us in to flood the fire. This was done but as soon as the door was opened and air got inside, the windows fell out and silver cigarette cases, vestas (ornate matchboxes) and other valuables from the window display ended up on the pavement. Being a 'gentleman's son' – and a former policeman, of course – I passed them by! We finished up at about three in the morning, deadbeat and wet through. But I felt very proud of myself, despite a very hesitant start to my first real fire.

By Whitsuntide that year, I'd found my feet and almost considered myself a seasoned fireman. On the Sunday I was showing a visitor from Salisbury, Rhodesia, around the engine room when suddenly the bells started ringing. The headgear was ablaze at the City and Suburban Mine, the implications of which were obviously very serious. Away we went at about three in the afternoon and did not return until the early hours of the next morning – which was Whit Monday when I was scheduled for duty at the Turfontein Race Course. Despite feeling very tired, I managed to get there and report in uniform for duty just before the races started. As I was standing by the rail, a punter came up to me and asked if I was having a bet on the next race. I said I only had about ten shillings. He told me to put all my money on a certain horse. 'If you lose, see me after the race and I'll refund every penny to you,' he said.

I decided to take a gamble – literally – and did as the man suggested. My horse romped home but I forget how much I won. As arranged, I met my benefactor at the same place after the race was over and started thanking him. He cut me short and told me to put half my earnings on another horse for the next race. I did so and backed another winner. The man had made me promise not to mention the tips he gave me to anyone else. I kept that promise. I don't remember how much I won that day, but I was very pleased with myself and, despite my tiredness, went home with a spring in my step. The party who had given me these tips was a complete stranger and I can only guess that he had some reason to be very grateful to a member of the fire brigade.

The long day wasn't over. Arriving back at the station, I was detailed to attend a large dance at the German Club that night. What a time I had dancing with all those nice girls! However, I didn't neglect my other duties and there was no fire. Escorted by several girls and just a few of their partners, I returned to the station in the early morning with a large bunch of flowers tucked into my tunic and, instead of wearing my round sailor cap and carrying my helmet, wearing my big brass helmet. The gladiator had returned in triumph with a bevy of fair maidens suitably rescued.

My colleagues of the Fire Brigade were a fine gang of fellows, always pulling jokes on each other. There was the time some of them unscrewed the comb of one man's helmet: that is, the part that sticks out on the top. Inside they placed a well-smoked kipper. Days later we had the regular Saturday inspection of kit which had to be arranged on each fireman's peg. The Chief Officer lifted the doctored helmet off the peg to examine it and was immediately assaulted by the smell. 'Good Lord!' he exclaimed. 'What have you been doing with your helmet? Are you too lazy to go outside at night?' The same man was the victim of another stinking ruse. Some Gorgonzola cheese was rubbed around the leather lining of his helmet. The alarm went off that night and we duly attended a fire. It was pretty warm and, what with the heat and the sweat pouring down the man's face, he began to smell – putting it mildly. The next thing I heard was a shout from one of the men holding the branch nozzle with him, 'You dirty bastard!' When anyone passed the poor devil, who appeared completely oblivious to the problem, they grabbed their noses muttering 'Whew'.

I shall never forget my first experience of escape drill. The escape ladder was eighty feet high when fully extended. The drill procedure was that the crew went to the top of the building against which the ladder was extended. One man, prostrate on the roof, had to be picked up by his rescuer and carried over his shoulders across the roof, before climbing over the coping and on to the escape ladder. Then came the eighty-foot descent. It was quite an easy matter for Tim, my half-section, to pick me up and sling me across his shoulder, surmount the coping and descend the ladder. But when it came for me to do the same with Tim who was heavily built and all of six-and-half feet, I was stumped. The Second Officer, in charge of the drill, relented just sufficiently to allow Tim to stand up and lean over my shoulders. He must have weighed about fourteen stone. I was also given a hand in the precarious transfer from coping to escape ladder. But when I started the descent with my knees shaking, Tim did nothing to improve matters by muttering, 'You bloody weakling, let me fall and I'll make bloody sure you'll come with me.' I was very thankful when I reached the ground but, after that first knee-trembling experience, I regained confidence and even looked forward to escape drills.

When the occasion demanded, the Brigade would put on a display of rescue work. I always seemed to land the part of the damsel in distress, wearing women's clothes and standing tearfully at a window waiting for the brave fireman to come up the escape and rescue me. I'm sure there's no need to report the lack of consoling words or the complete absence of tender concern shown by my gallant rescuer in response to my falsetto cries for help. I was treated like a sack of coal – much to the amusement of the audience.

Each man took his turn on duty in the watch room where every incident had to be recorded in the Occurrence Book. After doing the watch room night shift, a sort of bonus was to carry out duties at Johannesburg's several theatres and music halls. After checking that all the exit doors were in working order, the drill was to move on to the dressing rooms to ensure that none of the performers were smoking. The actors were usually too smart to be caught out but, should you happen to catch a sweet damsel with a cigarette between her lips, she would invariably wriggle out of censure and with fluttering eyelashes, get the better of a pliant officer!

Once the show was actually under way, the fireman's duty was to station himself in the wings, next to the telephone, so that in the event of fire he could immediately be in touch with the Fire Station.

It was almost inevitable that during my service in the Fire Brigade I should fall in love with many of those delightful actresses while listening to their singing or watching them dance. And if I was at the theatre on duty and witnessing a melodrama, I often had to restrain myself from rushing on to the stage and giving the villain a crack over the head with my fireman's axe, every time the script demanded he play rough with my heroine of the moment.

After serving in Johannesburg for several months, I was given the opportunity of joining the Pretoria Fire Brigade commanded by Captain Berrinton. There was a better chance of quick promotion so I decided to go there. Life in Pretoria was much the same except for one thing: there were not half as many fires. The Fire Station was alongside the old jail and if you peered over the wall, you could see the shed in which the condemned prisoners were hanged.

I remember the morning six Chinese men were to be hanged. Looking over the wall, we saw them being marched along to the shed and, about an hour later, being carried out. They got their just deserts since, as a gang, they had brutally carried out the murder of several residents.

Whilst in the Brigade I met an old friend whom I had known in Cape Town before the Boer War. A pork butcher by trade and a first class sausage and brawn maker, he was raising pigs on a farm he'd taken over in Witbank where he was slaughtering twice a week to supply the mines with pork sausages and brawn. He was looking for a partner with a few pounds and promised that in a very short period the modest investment would translate into a small fortune.

I fell for the idea, resigned from the service and left for Witbank to become a pork butcher. Well, not quite. My job was to ride around the mines getting orders. The next day I would assist with the slaughter and help in the butchery making the sausages and brawn. Then came the deliveries when I would hitch up our two horses to an American delivery cart and off I'd go on my rounds. It was always very late when I got back to the farm because of my habit of stopping off too long, talking and drinking tea with my customers.

Things seemed to be well for a while and then the time came when the pigs contracted measles from somewhere or other. That settled it: all the pigs were condemned as being unfit for human consumption and had to be destroyed. Again my hopes of making a fortune had flown out of the window – or rather 'Gone to the Pigs!'

# CHAPTER SEVEN

## Natal Rebellion – 1906

The rebellion had started in Natal and the Rand magnate, the late Sir Abe Bailey, was providing the finance for the formation of a small force raised in Johannesburg and called 'The Yorks and Lancs' or 'The Rosebuds'. Off I went to Johannesburg where I offered my services and was swiftly accepted. There was little or no military drilling demanded as most of the men had seen previous service, either in the Boer War or in one of the Southern African police forces.

We left Johannesburg by train for Natal where we detrained at, I think, Dundee. After obtaining transport we marched off, passing a number of places that had featured prominently during the Boer War such as Helpmekaar and Nurandhla until we arrived at Mapumulo.

The rebellion had been sparked off by the imposition of a poll tax in January by the Natal government although many said this was just an excuse to covering smouldering and wide-ranging discontent among the Zulu whose traditional homeland was being increasingly invaded. The ring-leader of the uprising, Bhambata, had already been disposed of, together with several hundred of his followers, at Mome Gorge early in June, but there were hundreds of the rebels still operating near Mapumulo and Thrings Post, situated on the road to Stanger. From Mapumulo, General McKenzie decided to drive up the Impanzi Valley.

If I remember correctly, his force consisted of units of the Transvaal Scottish, Natal Carbineers, 'The Rosebuds' and artillery, although many other forces had participated earlier – the Umvoti Mounted Rifles, Natal Field Artillery, Natal Mounted Police and Durban Light Infantry to name a few. Identifying other units to add to the 'motley', the five hundred men collectively known as the Transvaal Mounted Rifles were drawn from the Imperial Light Horse, South African Light Horse, the Johannesburg Mounted Rifles and the Scottish Horse. A day or two before we set out, a man named Veal employed by the Roads Department turned up at Mapumulo on a bicycle. He was warned not to ride on to Stanger as several bands of rebels were believed to be operating along the way. But he wouldn't listen. He reckoned he was well known to the natives in that part of the country and they wouldn't trouble him. So off he went.

The next day we moved out. Arriving near a large deserted native village, we rested beside a small stream. Some of the troops had gone right up to the village and suddenly one of them shouted and summoned those of us who were nearby. We joined him to find the mutilated remains of a white man. Alive, he had been a big man. Now his head was missing, his right arm cut off at the elbow (and missing), the soles of his feet cut off. He had been chopped down from the top of the spine to where the kidneys had been and savaged in other places. A thorough search of the village was carried out and an old woman – who must have been getting on for a hundred years – was discovered. Through her it was confirmed that the remains were those of Mr Veal. A message was heliographed to General Duncan McKenzie who was with the mounted troops on our left. We took turns in digging a grave with native hoes, the remains being covered with a blanket meanwhile. Shortly after, a man turned up with a camera and wanted to take a photo of the remains to send home to Kier Hardie, the Member of Parliament who had been asking questions in Westminster about why so few Zulu prisoners had been taken. No sooner had I lifted the blanket for the photo than General McKenzie turned up with his Staff Officer and a padre. The man who had taken the photo was told to destroy it.

After we had buried the remains and the padre had said a few words, we assembled and in open order climbed something of a rise. We had not gone far when the rebels who'd been hiding in the bush started up. All of them had shields and assegais of course but among them were a couple with guns. We fired a volley and downed dozens of them before the survivors were off like rabbits.

During the Impanzi Valley fight, the last of any great import, I regret to say one or two women were shot by accident, through running with their menfolk into the bush. One of our men found a dead woman with a child tied on her back. The child, a female about nine months old, was alive and unharmed. The trooper took charge of the infant and carried her until we were ordered out of the valley. He was allowed to ride back to camp on the gun carriage with the little girl and kept her in his tent with the other men that night, feeding her on tinned milk and nursing her when she cried for attention. The following morning he was summoned by the Staff Officer and told to hand over the child. She would be sent to Stanger and cared for by the Sisters of Nazareth there. He pleaded to be allowed to take the child to his wife in Johannesburg and promised to bring up the child until she was old enough to decide her own future. The officer couldn't allow this and so the baby was sent to Stanger by the next convoy, the man going with the child to hand her over in person to the nuns.

The men that had seen Veal's dismembered remains were very bitter and showed no mercy to the rebels. I recall walking along a gorge where we knew lots of the enemy were hiding. We were in open order, looking behind rocks and other possible hiding places. I found myself a little ahead of the rest of my unit. There was a shout: 'Me Christian boy, boss, me Christian boy!' Looking back, there was one of the rebels, dancing about and brandishing his shield and assegais. Taffy Harry, one of my mates responded, 'Christian Boy be damned, you bugger, I'll give you Christian Boy!' Taffy charged and bayoneted the native through the chest.

Soon after this, native policemen (there were many serving with us) were sent out to all the districts to inform the remaining rebels that if they came in and surrendered no further fighting would take place. A wire enclosure was erected to hold all those who surrendered. Dozens of them had worked on the Rand as waiters or in other jobs. I spoke to several of them and asked the reason for leaving the Rand, coming south and joining the rebellion. They all told the same story. Messengers sent from Zululand had ordered them to return home by a certain date. If they failed to do so, they would be killed if and when they ever did return.

With the rebellion over, it was decided to disband all the volunteers. We marched to Stanger and took the train from there to Durban and camped at Congella. After spending two or three days in Durban where the inhabitants feted us, we entrained for Johannesburg and were formally disbanded.

I went to see the chief of the Johannesburg Fire Brigade, hoping to rejoin, but there were no vacancies. He advised me to return to Rhodesia where a brigade was about to be formed in Bulawayo. With my service in the BSA

Police plus my experience as a fireman, I stood a good change of heading up the new unit. Armed with an introductory letter for the Bulawayo Mayor, Colonel Baxendale, from the Johannesburg Fire Master, I bade my friends goodbye and, at the beginning of September, once more took train for the land of promise.

1. Above.                  'Bunny' with lion he shot

2. Below.    Victoria Falls about 1908.   Trooper 'Bunny' Rabbetts seated on left

3.      'Bunny' Rabbetts in WW II uniform

4. A Rhodes Memorial Service, Salisbury, early 1950s. 'Bunny' Rabbetts on left
in front of statue of Rhodes in Jameson Avenue

5. Veterans of the South African War formed the guard of honour for the
Governor-General, Lord Dalhousie, when he attended a Battle of Britain
Service at St Mary's Cathedral, Salisbury. 'Bunny' Rabbetts third from right.

Photos 4 and 5  from *Rhodesia Herald*

# CHAPTER EIGHT

## BSA Police 1906-1911

In Bulawayo I booked into the old Queen's Hotel where I soon met up with a few of the policemen I'd served with. That night we crossed the Market Square to the Central Hotel where a singsong took place almost every night. It was well patronised by the Force and about that time Joe Phelan, ex-police and the man who was supposed to have held up the coach carrying the Killarney Mine gold, was one of the barmen there and – strangely perhaps – something of a hero.

I remember one of the artistes had 'R.A.M.' behind her name and whether this was meant to claim membership of the Royal Academy of Music, I can't say. But this particular evening the Master of Ceremonies had banged on the table and announced the lady as the next turn. She appeared on the stage and waited for the noise to stop before starting her song, which I think was called 'Bluebell'. As the noise continued, one of the audience yelled, 'Give the poor cow a chance!' The lady, not to be beaten, retorted, 'Thank you, I am pleased to see there is one gentleman in the audience!' The Central was a great place and the venue of many a rough house.

The following morning I went to see Colonel Baxendale who had the 'Blue Brand' mineral water factory. I presented him with my introductory letter from Johannesburg which he read – and laughed out loud, 'Come along, I'll show you the Fire Brigade!' With this, he took me to the Town Police Station where the fire machines were kept. As we entered the courtyard, he announced, 'This is the Fire Station.' I looked around and all I could see was an old manual pump, a hose reel and some buckets of sand. We had a talk and he promised that when the Bulawayo Municipality could afford proper fire appliances for the town, he would see I got the job as Chief of the Brigade. He advised me to rejoin the Force in the meantime. I thought I would look for a job in mining rather than take his advice. But that very same day – catching up on the social scene, as it were – I went to the station to witness the train leaving for the south. On the platform I ran into Major Straker whom I'd known in Mashonaland and who was with another officer whose name I've forgotten. The Major asked me what I'd been doing since leaving the Force. I gave him a quick review of my movements over the last two years and he asked me to come and see him at the camp the next morning. Major Straker must have been in contact with Salisbury because when I kept the appointment he said that I could re-enlist without delay and that I could leave that night for Salisbury. It was an invitation I hadn't really been expecting but I quickly accepted.

To my surprise there were half-a-dozen raw recruits on the overnight train who had come out from the Old Country to join the Force. The mule wagon customarily met us at the station in Salisbury and on arrival at camp we lined up in front of RSM Blatherwick's house. Jimmy came out but took no notice of me until he had spoken to the other men. He handed the recruits over to a sergeant – who, I think was 'Dicky' Green DCM. Then he came to me, shook me by the hand, said how pleased he was to see me back and then invited me in for a cup of tea.

I met many of the old hands who seemed pleased to see me again and I soon settled down to the old life. Although I was not treated as a recruit, I had to formally pass out with the newcomers who were then completing their training. After a couple of months doing uninteresting patrols, I was sent to Bulawayo on transfer.

The first thing I was put on to there was a CID job. Goods that had been off-loaded at Bembezi Siding, consigned to recipients working on the mines in the district, were being stolen from the siding. The simple reason for the thefts was that there was no one stationed at the siding to receive the goods or take care of them after they'd been dumped off the train. I first had to go to the station at Bulawayo where a whisky case filled with bottles of water and a sugar sack filled with sand were labelled and addressed to Mr Rabbetts, Lonely Mine.

After I'd seen the goods loaded into the van, I returned to camp and dressed up in old civilian clothes. I had a team of three native policemen also in civvy garb. At nightfall we boarded the train for Bembezi where I saw to the off-loading of my goods and their placement with other goods beside the track. We took our blankets and concealed ourselves in the bush, posted one of my team to watch the siding, and to wake me up should he see anyone interfering with the goods. Nothing happened that night. In the morning I went off to the Bembezi Police Camp, telling my men to keep out of sight as much as possible but to keep an eye on the goods.

Returning that evening, we positioned ourselves as before. At about two in the morning I was awakened when a native was seen going along the track casually inspecting the different goods. I watched the thief pick up my bag of sugar which had been placed a little away from the other goods. I whispered to my boys to let him get away with the sack. We would follow him, hoping he would be going to the nearby Fingo Location where we might uncover evidence of earlier thieving.

My team grabbed their sticks and knobkerries and off we went, keeping in the shadows of the moonlit night as much as possible. Our quarry with the sack seemed to be heading straight for the village when all of a sudden I came a cropper over a log or something and couldn't avoid making a hell of a row. The native stopped, realised he was being followed, dropped the sack and ran. I shouted to the native police to get after him and off they went, with myself coming up far behind. As they closed on the thief, one of my men threw his knobkerrie at the native's legs, bowling him over like a rabbit. Before he could regain his feet, my boys were on him and, after a bit of a struggle, had him handcuffed. Never have I seen a knobkerrie used so effectively. We returned to Bulawayo with our prisoner that morning.

Shortly after this I was transferred to Wankie. What a hole it was in those days. Almost always there was someone down with blackwater fever or malaria. One of the least desirable jobs for the policemen there was meeting the northbound train that arrived at about ten o'clock at night. It was no picnic negotiating the path down the kopje from the camp to the station. On the descent one had to walk by the butcher's shop, run by a former policeman, Jack Osborne. He had a caged leopard guarding his shop and the damn thing put the wind up anyone passing by and swinging a hurricane lamp.

One night when it was my turn for duty, the train was late so to pass the time we held an impromptu concert at the old station hotel managed by Cooney Wood. We carried on singing songs and imbibing until past midnight. At last the train arrived, was attended to and sent on its way to Victoria

Falls.

But there was always time for another song and another nightcap before I set off back to camp. I managed to get past the leopard but tiredness really set in before the last climb. It was time to have a rest. Blowing out the lamp, I used it as a pillow and off I went to sleep. I was awakened early in the morning by the sounds of shots being fired near the compound and much shouting from the natives.

I staggered into camp to find that the NCO-in-charge, Sergeant Major Godfrey, had just sent some of the native police down to the compound to find out what all the excitement was about. They returned with the news that the compound manager, Mr Hammerton, had shot a lion. The beast's spoor was found later at the butcher's shop, then along the path next to the hospital and on towards the compound. I'd been sleeping less than fifty yards from the lion's route. I resolved that in future I'd celebrate the train's arrival and departure with nothing stronger than tea!

Soon after my narrow escape, a telegram arrived authorising the arrest of the alleged robber, Joe Phelan, who was known to have left the train at Matetsi, just north of us but thirty miles south of Victoria Falls. He was wanted in Bulawayo to answer a charge of Contempt of Court and was thought to be making for German South West Africa up the Zambezi via the Caprivi Strip. I was to accompany Sergeant Major Godfrey on the chase and our plan was to try and intercept Phelan at Kazungula which was on the Zambezi at the Bechuanaland Border. We rode out with two native constables and a pack mule. First we made for Geise's Farm at Pandamatenka and then carried on towards Kazungula. One of the constables volunteered that he knew a short cut to a village – I've forgotten its name – from whence a track led to Matetsi.

It was about four in the afternoon when we neared the village and heard shots. We cantered closer to see a white man throw something into the grass. I recognised Bob Johnson, another doubtful character from Bulawayo. Godfrey asked him right out where Phelan was and was told that he was out shooting. We demanded to be shown where they were camped. Johnson led us to the village and showed us a hut inside of which we found a dozen un-muzzled dogs, guns and cases of ammunition. Johnson was asked for permits for the guns and ammunition and admitted he had none. We arrested him and settled down, waiting for Phelan to return. Then we heard natives singing along the track leading in to the village. Another European – not Phelan – headed up a gang carrying more cases of ammunition. He got a shock when Godfrey and I stepped out to meet him. His name was Keys and, with no permits, he was also put under arrest. We settled down again to await Phelan but he didn't turn up.

During the night, Godfrey decided to leave at daybreak for Matetsi with the two prisoners, Johnson and Keys, and with the village natives carrying the captured guns and ammunition. I was to remain in the village until another trooper was sent from Matetsi to assist me. Then we were to continue the pursuit to Kazungula. The constable I was left with hid my mule and remained out of sight to give Phelan the impression, should he return to the village, that we had all left.

Shortly after the others had gone, I heard the approach of a horse or mule and, on going outside the hut in which I'd been hiding, I came face to face with a mounted trooper. We hadn't met before but, as I was wearing an old helmet with a white puggaree, not police issue, I had the greatest difficulty convincing him that I was not Phelan (it was said I looked somewhat like him.) Eventually I showed him my police mule and the native policeman arrived to further confirm my identity.

The trooper had been sent from Victoria Falls as part of the hunt. I brought him up to date and suggested that he remain with me that day. I also sent a runner off with a report to Sergeant Major Godfrey. The Falls trooper had been warned that Phelan was a rough customer who would shoot if challenged. But I had known Phelan in Bulawayo and didn't think he would fire if he recognised me. The headman had been instructed to warn me as soon as Phelan was seen approaching the village.

Later on, we were sitting in the hut when the headman came running up saying, 'Nangu lo Boss'. The other trooper grabbed his rifle but I told him not to be a bloody fool and to remain in the hut whilst I went to meet Phelan. I came round another of the huts and there was Phelan with his shotgun at the ready. 'Hallo Joe,' I said very casually. Once he'd recovered from his shock, he asked me if I'd arrived with Godfrey the previous evening. Obviously he'd been watching the village for some time. I told him I had. He said he hadn't recognized me in my non-issue helmet. 'If I had, I would have surrendered myself to you, but not to that bastard Godfrey.'

Phelan had been up a tree all night and in the morning, after Godfrey had left with his captives, could not find out what had happened to his friends. And now he was suffering badly with fever. I got him to the hut, introduced him to the other trooper and – now that there was safety in numbers – told him he was under arrest. Then I put him to bed. His temperature was high so I treated him with some hot tea and aspirin and, after he had had a good sweat, I gave him a dose of quinine. He slept like a log until evening and said he felt much better after a meal of chicken stew.

That night I asked Phelan if he could manage to ride a mule. If so, we would start for Matetsi at daybreak with the other trooper and myself taking turns in walking and riding. We set off very early. I wanted to catch the train I knew was due at Matetsi at about noon. We were close to the railway track when I heard the train's whistle so I told Phelan to dismount and together we ran down the line to the station where the train was just pulling in. The other trooper was to take my mule and the pack mule to Native Commissioner Fuller at his camp and then ride his own mount back to Victoria Falls. Phelan and I reached the station just as Sergeant Major Godfrey and the other prisoners were boarding the train.

We all returned to Wankie without incident and the next morning Keys and Johnson were brought before the magistrate.They were fined and the ammunition and guns confiscated but Phelan had to be taken to Bulawayo for trial. I was to have another run-in with Joe Phelan a few months later.

Rabies had broken out in Northern Rhodesia so all dogs on our side of the border had to be muzzled as a precaution. Natives were warned to collect muzzles from the Native Commissioner's office and given plenty of time to obtain them. Then I was sent on an extended patrol to visit all villages southeast of Wankie right down to the Gwaai River. Any dogs I found un-muzzled were to be shot without question and for this job I was supplied with a shotgun and ammunition. It was an unpleasant business and I must have shot as many as eighty dogs. Pleasant or not, it was nothing to expect a medal for but I almost got shot myself. I had arrived at a squatter's pole and dagga homestead near the Gwaai River, occupied, if I remember aright, by a Dutchman, his wife and family. I had noticed several ferocious but un-muzzled dogs running about and politely informed the Dutchman what my duties were. His response was that if I shot one of his dogs, he would shoot me. His kind and loving wife backed him up. Then he explained why he was being so obstructive.

He asked me to go with him to a hut close by where he showed me the skin of a lion he had shot a couple of days before. He'd been sitting on the stoep with a couple of his children about sundown, when his wife happened to walk out from the room behind to join her husband. Looking out into the surrounding bush, she saw what she thought at first was a big dog. A switching tail made her change her mind – it was a lion. It seemed as if the huge cat was preparing to launch itself onto the verandah. She quietly went into the room, grabbed a gun, fired and hit the lion. From what the husband told me, his wife then promptly fainted! On hearing the shot, the dogs came barking from behind the homestead and baled up the badly wounded lion. The husband finished it off with another shot. He insisted that lions were very numerous in this neck of the woods to the extent that he was seriously thinking of moving closer to civilization. I certainly made no attempt to shoot his dogs.

Soon after this anti-rabies patrol, I was detailed to go on patrol with a very fine officer, Lieutenant Agar. He had a horse but I was riding a mule – and the devil of a beast it was too. We were no more than about six miles from Wankie, on the path to Pandamatenga and Geise's Farm, when my mule shied at something and threw me off. I landed on a boulder, hitting my spine so badly that I was unable to stand. Lieutenant Agar returned to Wankie, gathered up some natives and a stretcher and had me carried back to camp. I lay on my stomach for about a week and it was another two weeks before I could walk without assistance. Given the choice of a transfer to Victoria Falls or Fort Victoria, I chose Victoria Falls and arrived there a day or two later. In charge was dear old Henry Ford (not the motor man). My first patrol was up the south bank of the Zambezi as far as the border at Kazungulu, then down the old border road to the Kasuma Pans and Pandamatenga before turning east for the more familiar area around Matetsi and then up the railway line and home. It took some time to organize the native constable, the pack donkeys and my mule for the extended patrol so we left the station well after noon, planning to make our first night halt at the old drift. There was plenty of daylight left when we arrived and I decided to try to shoot something for the pot.

We'd not gone very far when my scout pointed out some buck grazing in a nearby vlei. Getting a bit closer, I took a shot at a small one and, more by luck than judgment, dropped it. The rest of the buck cleared off but as we reached the one I'd shot, my heart nearly stopped. Looking at the dead buck in the deepening twilight, I was almost certain I'd shot one of my pack donkeys. I remained unconvinced until I got back to my camp where my trophy turned out to be a young waterbuck. I still had a lot to learn amid all this wild life and during the night I kept a big fire going. Hippos were very numerous about here, coming from the river to graze in the immediate vicinity of our camp. In fact, I had to frighten them off with a shot or two.

We visited several villages on the way to the border at Kazungulu. At one kraal there was a native, whose name I have forgotten, but who had been Cecil Rhodes' servant and been granted certain privileges. One of these, I remember, was that he was allowed to have both a rifle and a shotgun.

On one occasion I got him to take me hunting guinea fowl. I was walking just in front of him when we heard a rustling noise behind. The next thing I knew was being pushed in the back and I almost fell on my face as my guide rushed past me. Regaining my balance, I looked behind to see a large mamba poised on its tail. Fortunately I had the shotgun in my hands and fired, blowing the snake's head off. It was all of twelve feet long. Cecil Rhodes' man had gone quite grey and I had certainly experienced a big fright. It didn't help to be told that when a mamba stands on its tail it can move quickly and that there was little doubt that it intended to strike one of us. Had it done so it would have been the end for the guide or for me – almost certainly me considering the position he'd left me in! However, luck was with us that day.

Another not quite so narrow an escape was when we had halted, to escape the midday sun, somewhere between Pandamatenka and Matetsi.

The donkeys and my mule were grazing close by on our left. I happened to glance to my right towards a belt of trees and there, on top of a small ant heap just a few yards away, was a lion lying down and very obviously contemplating the donkeys as its lunch. I had used up almost all my rifle ammunition and my shotgun would not have been the best defence. Discretion and valour and all that – so I decided to call off lunch, pack up and trek, leaving Leo to have the field to himself.

A man named Cummings took up this part of the country for farming soon afterwards. I heard that his son subsequently shot over a hundred lions in a period of just a few years. The vicinity of Kasuma Pans is now of course the Wankie Game Reserve and home to many lions.

During my stay at Victoria Falls from 1907 to 1910, I must have done the aforementioned triangular patrol at least a couple of dozen times. Later in life I travelled many miles in Northern Rhodesia and Barotseland but I firmly believe that nowhere is there better game viewing, perhaps with the exception of elephant and rhino, than at Kasuma Pans.

Hippos below Kandahar Island threatened tourist visitors going up the Zambezi. Several canoes were upset with loss of life and the police were permitted to shoot a few to discourage the others. Ex-Trooper 'Baby' Richardson and another hunter, Walker, were likewise authorized.

There was the time I was enjoying a picnic on Kandahar Island with some visitors. Among them by the way, was a French baroness who later wrote to me in French from the different places she was visiting on her world tour. I had to get her letters translated by the chef at the hotel. By so doing, of course, he knew as much as I did about my affair and my lady's adventures – and he was not the most discreet of chefs! But we used to laugh at the address she put on her letters:

'Mons. Ra-Bbetts, Chef a la Police, Victoria Falls.'

I regret I never had the chance to accept her many invitations to visit her home on the Rue de Prone, Paris. But let me return to the island and our picnic.

After we'd finished our lunch, I heard hippos in the river. Looking downstream I saw some two hundred yards away the heads of two hippos above the water facing me. I took careful aim and fired from the prone position, not without some intention of impressing the tourists. I was sure I'd scored a hit but my targets just disappeared for something of an anti-climax. A week later Walker found a hippo in a trap he'd fixed up on one of their runs. The natives skinning the beast noticed a bad wound in the forehead and on closer examination there was my soft-nosed bullet flattened out on the skull. Had I used a solid round, no doubt it would have penetrated – but the poor hippo must have suffered a bad headache.

Another memorable hippo occasion came when it was my turn to go out with the boys to help bring in a big buck that had been shot by Trooper John Hutson who, incidentally, died a few years ago at Fort Victoria. As I'd been tempted into enjoying yet another singsong at the hotel with the guests, it was late in the afternoon before we set out to retrieve the meat. Hutson accompanied me. The dead buck was lying off the track near the old Livingstone drift where I thought I'd earlier shot one of my pack donkeys. It was fairly dark by the time we got to the point on the path where Hutson had put a branch to indicate the position of the dead buck.

I'd just dismounted when Hutson whispered, 'There's a hippo,' pointing at the same time. I looked but could see no movement, only something that looked like a mound. 'It's nothing,' I said but he insisted that it was a hippo. As I was not carrying a rifle, I asked him for his and moved forward a little. I knelt down and, taking aim at what I thought might be the front part, fired. There was a noise like 'Hu' and the mound collapsed. I fired again. By now the boys were excited and so were Hutson and myself. We made some torches of dried grass, lit them and approached the beast. It turned out to be a cow hippo that had just been giving birth to a calf. Both were dead and I was very fed up about the whole thing.

One doesn't expect such large animals to be encountered 'lying in wait' as it were. Another time I was camped at the drift not far away and, when it was almost dark, I went out with a boy hoping to get a shot at a hippo. Nearing one of their runs, I heard the unmistakable sound of a hippo just leaving the water, so got behind a tree. I could just make out its head and forequarters coming out of the run when I fired. It grunted as it was hit and flopped back into the river but that set off one hell of a noise in the vlei behind me. Several hippos that had been grazing stampeded for the water and I was between them and their objective. I flattened myself against the tree and could have smacked one of the hippos on the back as it dashed by me into the river. The native with me shared my very narrow escape.

I had an arrangement with Ruby, the runner at the hotel who was also in charge of the boats, that if I bagged a hippo, he would go up the river with boys in a canoe, get it to the bank, and skin it. The hide would be cut into strips and sold to the ready tourist market. Ruby and I would then go fifty-fifty on the proceeds. I told Ruby about my latest kill. From the noise it had made in the river, I knew it had been mortally wounded. Ruby searched, couldn't find it and chided me for wasting his time. Much later, he climbed down the gorge below the hotel and was driven back by the smell from a dead hippo wedged in some rocks. We presumed it was the one I had shot and that it had been washed over the Falls.

Another time I saw what I thought was the head of a hippo showing above water. I fired and hit my target. As I was to be away for a couple of days, I sent a message to Ruby that I had badly wounded a hippo. On my return I made straight for Ruby, anxious for my share of the proceeds. His response was colourful: 'It ain't a bleedin' hippo, it's a bleedin' croc. I left it up the river on some rocks.' Not wanting to entirely miss the opportunity of some pocket money, I got some boys and a canoe from him and went upstream. We needed no compass to guide us to the croc – the smell was enough. However, with extravagant promises made to the boys, we got it to the bank. It was all of fourteen feet long. I had it skinned with the head still on and the jaws forced open, kept in that position with a stick. I wanted to peg it out in the camp where I could keep an eye on my trophy but my colleagues weren't supportive. Eventually, I got the skin dried and quite a few visitors came to camp to see it.

That put me in mind of a good scheme. I had signed a few chits at the hotel and I suggested to the manager that he could have the croc skin to hang at the front entrance of the hotel. It would be of interest to the tourists and might tempt them in for a drink. He fell for my suggestion and cancelled my cards – quite a fair amount. The skin was displayed and was fine during the dry season. But when the rains started, the skin started to shrivel and stink. It was taken down and sent back from whence it came – to the river.

# CHAPTER NINE

## Phelan and the Badlands

Earlier I promised to recall my subsequent encounters with Joe Phelan who had joined the Force in mid-1904, some nine months after my first period of police service in Mashonaland. I first came across him in person when he was working as a barman in Bulawayo, after he had somehow wriggled out of his alleged involvement in the Killarney Gold Robbery and been discharged from the Force. Then, as I've said, our paths crossed, literally, when I was stationed at Wankie. After I had arrested him and sent him to Bulawayo, he managed once again to escape the clutches of justice.

Now there were reports that Phelan and a couple of other desperados were up to no good in and around 'No Man's Land', the Caprivi Strip near Kazungulu. Information obtained by natives who periodically visited relatives in the barely-administered German territory (known formally as the Caprivi Zipfel), was that Phelan and his gang were playing hell with the locals, stealing their cattle and even going so far as to shoot any native who tried to stop them.

Some time after we got wind of what Phelan and his friends were up to, I went on patrol to Kazungulu accompanied by Trooper Earl Simmonds. It was his first patrol from the Falls and he was very proud of his new sporting .303 rifle. We had paused for lunch near one of the villages when my colleague took the opportunity to try out his new acquisition. After his shooting trip, we saddled up and proceeded on our way, riding side by side with myself very slightly ahead. Simmonds had the rifle across the pommel of his saddle, the barrel pointing towards my back. Suddenly there was a shot. How it missed me, God alone knows. My half-section must have omitted to unload the round in the breech and had unintentionally pressed the trigger. Poor Simmonds – how upset he was when it dawned on him just how close he'd been to shooting me. I wasn't too impressed with the experience either! We arrived at Kazungulu and camped in the familiar spot, under the big 'sausage' tree, on the river bank. Simmonds was keen to do a bit more shooting. I was not at all inclined to go with him and stretched out on my blanket. Presently one of the boys told me a canoe was coming down the river from German territory. I got up to see a white man standing in the stern of the frail craft, directing his boys towards our camp. There came a shout. 'Is that you, Bunny?' I recognised the brogue: it was Joe Phelan. I replied and shortly afterwards the canoe pulled in at the bank and out jumped Joe. After the usual small talk, I ordered up tea and some food.

Phelan had hardly sat down when one of his canoe boys came towards me jabbering his head off. Others of the crew were in close support. I couldn't make out what the spokesman was trying to say but Phelan evidently got the message. In an instant he jumped up, drew his revolver – one of the pair he had stuck in his belt – and ordered the boys back to the canoe. They ran like rabbits but Phelan did nothing to explain the interruption to me.

Phelan then asked me if I had seen Jack Friend. I knew that Friend was the Filabusi gold miner who – the Bulawayo scuttlebutt alleged – had been Phelan's accomplice in the hold-up at Killarney Mine. No, I hadn't seen or heard of him recently. I didn't let on to Joe that it was fairly common knowledge at Victoria Falls that the two of them were among the ne'er-do-wells on the Caprivi Strip.

Phelan then told me the following tale – with not a trace of conscience or shame about what he was virtually confessing to a policeman. It appears that Friend and he had quarrelled and both had gone their different ways hunting elephant. Friend, claimed Phelan, had run short of ammunition, gone back to Phelan's hut and helped himself to all the ammunition he could lay his hands on. When Phelan returned and found out from his camp followers what had happened, he swore he would shoot Friend on sight. Soon after, locals spotted Friend in the vicinity and reported to Phelan who then, with the help of natives, brought his former partner back to the hut and tied him up for the night. Phelan told Friend that he wouldn't shoot him as promised and that in the morning he would only cut off his ears and set him adrift in a canoe. But one of his natives had released Friend during the night. Phelan said quite openly that the native in question would never set anyone else free, by which I presumed he'd shot Friend's liberator. Was that what

Phelan's men had been trying to report to me before they'd been herded back to the river?

I'd found myself in a most peculiar situation. There was little or no hard proof to support the crimes allegedly committed by Phelan and/or his gang on either side of the border. On the other hand, the former trooper seemed quite convinced that the German administration, such as it was, would sooner or later formally request the Rhodesian authorities to send policemen into the Caprivi to arrest him and the rest of the gang. I pleaded with Phelan to let me take him back to Bulawayo and sort matters out once and for all. But it was no good – he wouldn't listen.

I asked him to tell me the truth about the Killarney hold-up but he just laughed and said I should pull his other leg. So I enquired about another story going the rounds in Victoria Falls, concerning Joe and a Greek trader who had gone into the Caprivi to buy cattle, intending to run the beasts across the Zambezi into Northern Rhodesia where there was a ready market, but illegal in that cross-border cattle movement was not allowed then.

Phelan said that the Greek had come to his camp and, after having taken tea, Joe had asked the visitor what he up to.

'Trading cattle with the natives,' the Greek replied. He produced two hundred and fifty pounds in cash to prove his point.

'Why buy them, why not just take them from the natives?' countered Phelan, telling me this with no trace of shame.

'How can I do that?' asked the Greek.

'Get the Induna (headman) and tie him up.'

'I don't know how to tie anyone up,' said the Greek innocently.

'Let me show you.'

The Greek stood up and Phelan got a reim, twisted it around his legs and arms and, when he had him tied, gave him a wallop on the jaw, knocking him unconscious. Then, Phelan boasted, he'd called his boys who put the intruder in a canoe and set it adrift to float down the Zambezi. Joe didn't bother to mention that the Greek's cash had been left behind! Natives on the north bank spotted the canoe the next day and went after it. They must have got a shock on finding a man trussed up in the boat. By this time the Greek was almost off his head but they got him ashore. The chief had him carried to hospital in Livingstone where he eventually recovered. Later he made a statement to the magistrate.

Joe's story, in a very backhanded way, was a tribute to his police training and the rules of evidence. I could just imagine him telling the magistrate – if it ever came to that – how he had taken it upon himself to prevent the Greek from trading diseased cattle over the border. And he'd made no bones about telling me the whole story, knowing full well that I could do nothing about the 'crimes' he'd confessed to without corroboration. It was hardly surprising that he'd wriggled out of all the charges brought against him by the full force of the law back in Bulawayo.

Phelan didn't stay long. He finished his tea, said goodbye and was paddled upstream back to German territory. I never saw him again but tales of his doings regularly floated down to the river to the Falls.

Almost the last of these stories was the report from a native of his death. There was a criminal named Moodey, also at large in the Caprivi. It seems that Moodey and Phelan had worked together as hunters but had quarrelled. They threatened to shoot each other on sight. Some time later, a native reckoned he saw Phelan on the path leading to Moodey's hut. The native ran and warned Moodey who picked up his rifle and left the hut. The native started to follow Moodey but was told go back as the intention was only to shoot buck. Later a shot was heard, after which Moodey returned to the hut. The native asked him where he had left the buck and was told it had been a miss. But Moodey was such a good shot that the native didn't believe him. The following morning this same native went to get water from the river and saw blood spoor on the path with marks of something having been dragged into the reeds. He followed the tracks and among the reeds came across the body of Phelan lying on his back.

All of this was recorded in a formal statement made to me at the Victoria Falls police station. True to form where the Irishman was concerned, there was never anything to substantiate the demise of Joe Phelan.

Back to the patrol we'd been on when Joe Phelan had surprised me at Kazungula. Of course Simmonds had been out playing with his new rifle the whole time Joe had been with me and had missed the 'confession'. In retrospect I don't think Joe would have been so forthcoming had my colleague been present to witness the story. And I'd made no secret of the fact that I wasn't alone on patrol – which perhaps explained why my visitor had left rather abruptly once he'd established that I'd had neither sight nor sound of his quarry, Jack Friend.

Simmonds and I completed the upstream leg of our patrol and started back for the Falls. At a village about eleven miles downstream from Kazungulu, we made camp for the night. The local chief came and reported that two white men had arrived at his village having been ferried across the Zambezi. One of the men, he informed me, was none other than Jack Friend. It seemed that the pair were making for the Falls so I decided to let them get ahead of us. When we got to camp I reported to Henry Ford, leaving my NCO to decide what to do about Friend, if indeed it was him, and the other man. They were thought to have made camp down by the old water tanks, about half a mile from the station. The next day, Friday, there was no sign of them however.

It must have been the following Sunday when a runner arrived with a letter from the Livingstone magistrate. A prisoner by the name of McClusky had escaped from the jail there and we were to be on the watch for him. We discussed the matter and reckoned that it was more than likely that Friend's companion was the wanted McClusky. Trooper Billie Walters was detailed to patrol up to Kazungulu, from where I'd just come. Billie was to warn all the locals to report immediately should they see strangers, and to keep a weather eye open himself, of course.

Meanwhile I saddled the only horse available, old George, and set off with a native policeman for the old Livingstone Drift again. There we searched in vain for signs of a canoe having been pulled upon the bank. What we did find were fresh tracks apparently made by someone who had landed during the night. We followed the spoor, which led back in the direction of the Falls. In some places it was clear that the person had removed his boots and gone for a short distance without them – very suspicious! We traced the spoor right up to the railway track just above the bridge. Soper, the bridge attendant, had his hut there. I asked Soper if he was aware of anyone having crossed the bridge from south to north during the night. He hadn't seen anyone but the patent alarm he'd fixed up to tell if anyone was trying to cross from either side had been interfered with. Back at the station I duly reported and my conclusions – such as they were – were sent across to the magistrate in Livingstone.

Much later we heard that a Native Department messenger in Livingstone had been deputized as a special constable and sent up towards Kazungulu along the north bank. Before he got there, the locals told him that three white men had passed on their way to Kazungulu. Further on he was informed that these same men were negotiating at a nearby village for a canoe to take them over to German territory. By the time he got to the village, the men were well across the Zambezi, well on their way back to the Badlands.

The incidents of those few days graphically illustrated the problem of policing this corner of Southern Rhodesia.

When Billie Walters returned from the fruitless jaunt to Kazungulu, he was sick with fever. Billie occupied the hut next to mine and it had an annex leading from the sleeping quarters. This night Corporal Ford and I left poor old Billie in bed and went to the hotel to enjoy the company of the tourists. We didn't get back until after midnight – and found Billie sitting up with his shotgun in his hands and about a dozen cartridges on the bed. His fevered state had little to with his sickness. What had happened was this: Shortly after we'd left, Billie had heard a noise outside the annex. Then the noise came from inside the annex. On sitting up, Billie found himself staring at a lion – and the lion was gazing at Billie! The trooper was paralysed and unable to move but the lion just did an about turn and left. Shortly after, Billie heard galloping hooves on the path leading down towards the station and correctly identified the old mule that belonged to Walker, the hunter, and slept outside the stables every night.

'Editor's Note: It is unfortunate that the author says little about co-operation – or its lack – with the Bechuanaland Border Police (BBP), the Barotseland Native Police (BNP) or the authorities in German South West Africa at this time. Nor does he mention that the police station at Victoria Falls was opened only a year or so before he was posted there, the larger BSA Police presence being at Wankie'.

The mule was found the next morning standing on the Falls Bridge with its rump all torn. It seemed that the lion had gone for the mule as it was galloping off in panic from the stables. The next day, Ford and I decided to put our mattresses, blankets and rifles on top of the stable that night and lie up, hoping Leo would return and we'd get a shot at him. We reckoned we were entitled to a nightcap before mounting sentry duty on the stable roof and went down to the hotel where, I'm afraid, we made no secret of our coming adventure. With a beer bottle of absinthe – which I'd been taught to drink by the French Countess – to keep us warm on a cold night, as it must have been June or July, we returned to camp and climbed on the roof. Wrapped in our blankets, we took to the bottle. It was then that we heard someone snoring. Looking along the roof, we noticed another blanket-covered form and concluded that Walker must have heard of our plans to rendezvous with Leo and had decided he would also join the party.

My colleague must have already been dozing when I heard the cracking of the thorn bush fence in front of us. I nudged Ford at the same time as the lion roared and Henry, being on the edge of the roof, almost rolled off. We couldn't see where the lion went after it bounded away which was a problem but, after finishing off the contents of the bottle, we plucked up enough courage to make for our huts. The following morning at the seven o'clock stable parade we found not only Walker but also Baby Richardson still asleep on the roof. Told about the lion, they admitted they hadn't heard it roar. It's hard to say what they'd been drinking – not absinthe!

On one occasion Ford had saddled up our old horse George to take the well-beaten track up to the drift. I happened to be in the office making out registration certificates for a couple of natives when drumming hooves interrupted my duties. Going outside to investigate, I saw Corporal Ford with his arms around George's neck and unable to stop his mount galloping headlong for the stables. Fortunately the stable doors were wide open and in went George, coming to a sudden stop at the manger. Henry went just a little bit further to end up in the manger. I helped him out and asked what had happened. 'Happened, be damned!' he said, 'I'll never go out for a ride on my own again without a rifle.' George had been trotting along nicely, as befitting his age, when without warning out of the bush in front bounded two lion cubs, fairly big, and then followed by the mother. 'Poor old George stopped short, turned almost in mid-air and made for home sweet home. How the hell I didn't fall off, I don't know. I grabbed the saddle and any damned thing I could lay hands on – his tail if I could've got hold of it! I lost my switch and my helmet and I just hope those damned lions haven't scoffed it.' My very chastened NCO got two or three men with rifles to go out with him seeking revenge on the lions but they had no luck. They did recover his switch and helmet. Visitors at the hotel were enthralled by the tale while Henry, having to tell the story repeatedly, was well compensated with liquid refreshment.

Some American tourists arrived at the Falls and within a few hours I was summoned by the hotel manager. One of the visitors was demanding that the police come down to investigate his sighting of lions in the Rain Forest. I had a quiet laugh to myself – lions didn't like the damp – but went down to the hotel to discover what had happened. The opening salvo went like this: 'Say, Constable, we people have travelled thousands of miles to see this goldarned waterfall. Me and my partner were hiking down to the Rain Forest when we saw these goldarned lions so we came back pronto. It's up to you guys – you're supposed to be keeping the peace – to hustle them lions out of it. Shoot them. Do what you like, but we ain't going back until they're gotten rid of.'

I tried to convince the Yank that lions had never been encountered in the Rain Forest. He wouldn't believe me and insisted that I go down and check. I did so. On nearing the Rain Forest I came on a troop of baboons. Satisfied that they were what he had seen, I went back to the hotel. In front of everyone I told him that his goldarned lions were only baboons. The other visitors were most amused and the Yank's leg was pulled mercilessly afterwards. But he had the last laugh. He wagered that he could lift up a dining-room chair with his nose, the gamble being the price of drinks all round. Several people, myself included, quickly took him up on his challenge. From out of his pocket he produced a small silk handkerchief, poked one end through the bottom of his nose and, tying the handkerchief round the back of a chair, lifted it up with no difficulty. He had a gold bridge in his nose!

A telegram arrived from the Officer Commanding at Wankie instructing me to report there and assist in escorting some two thousand pounds of hut tax proceeds to the Standard Bank in Bulawayo. Another trooper – I'll call him Smith – joined me at Wankie with the money packed in an ammunition box. I placed the box under the seat in our compartment. Once we were on our way, the conversation came round to Joe Phelan and the Killarney Mine business. Smith pointed out how easy it would be for us to throw the case out of the window and jump out after it when it got dark and the train was steaming along the Malinde Straight. It was very sandy next to the track and we wouldn't be hurt when we landed...

I got the wind up, honestly believing he was quite serious about the plan if I was to give him the slightest encouragement – and I've never altered that opinion. However, I told him not to be a damn fool. After having dinner in the saloon I returned to the compartment to check that everything was all right. Then someone invited the pair of us for a drink. Back in the saloon, I'm ashamed to relate (again) that we had one too many. Tim Ward, the train's chief steward (and later manager of the Falls Hotel), was always out for a joke. After wishing our drinking companions goodnight, Trooper Smith and I returned to our compartment and turned in. Next morning near Redbank Siding I awoke and the first thing I did was to check the ammunition box. It was missing.

My immediate thought was that Trooper Smith had dumped it out of the window somewhere. When I tackled him, he swore he hadn't touched it. We went looking in every compartment but no trace of the box could we find. Then I went to the saloon to see Tim Ward. He must have realised how worried I was and burst out laughing. Taking me to the ice chest, he showed me the missing ammunition case he'd placed there while we were too busy drinking the previous evening.

No sooner had I returned to the Falls than I was informed that I had been seconded to Matetsi as cattle inspector. Cattle from Barotseland were now being allowed into Southern Rhodesia but they had to undergo two months' quarantine at Matetsi. I was to go to Matetsi and have the old Native Commissioner's quarters made habitable for myself as well as for a veterinary surgeon who would be sent there to carry out inspections. I got the accommodation requirement out of the way and returned to the Falls. Two days later I boarded the train for Matetsi, knowing that it was to be my home for several months.

As the cattle arrived in the area from the other side of the Zambezi, they were driven into bush kraals that had been erected by the different owners of the herds. Several thousand head had already arrived and they'd not been there many days before lions made their presence known. Cattle were being taken night and day. Then the owners started putting poison into the many carcasses strewn around. Riding round one morning visiting cattle posts, I saw no less than eight dead lions, four outside one particular cattle kraal. During the quarantine period, many lions were shot besides those poisoned. Then East Coast Fever broke out and claimed hundreds of the cattle that had been saved from the lions!

The kraals were visited by several veterinary surgeons, among them the late Mr Hooper-Sharpe with whom I often teamed up to patrol the area. On one occasion we started on a fairly long tour going west from Matetsi and then north towards the Falls. We started off on mules, with native police and personal servants and half-a-dozen pack donkeys. Shortly after setting out, we encountered a Scotch cart hurrying in the opposite direction. In the cart was an injured white man who had been staying with Koonie Wood, the latter being in a farming partnership with the late Mr Westwood. The casualty had been badly mauled by a lioness and was being taken to catch the train for Wankie to receive medical attention. Lions had killed cattle on the Westwood farm and Wood and the visitor had unwisely decided on a spot of vengeance. They had some dogs and taking these with them, also a few locals – one of whom had been armed with a rifle – they set out to track the lions.

The native with the rifle was in front. Suddenly he saw a lion and lioness under a big tree, fired and – not surprisingly – missed. The lioness came for him. He turned and took to his heels, passing the visitor who was knocked flat by the lioness. As the man tried to protect his face, the lioness grabbed his arm. Fortunately the dogs intervened to worry the lioness and this gave Koonie a chance to get a shot in, killing the lioness.

There was little we could do to help the injured man – getting to Wankie swiftly was his best option – so we continued on our way. We saw plenty of big game later that morning but we wanted something small for the pot and a little later I shot a small wild pig. We stopped for lunch at the Sabahlesa River and afterwards followed the river to get to Matthysen's Farm. Hooper-Sharpe was riding in front with me close behind. Across the stream on my left I saw a couple of lions watching us intently. Dismounting, I aimed and fired. It sounded as if I had scored a hit but off went the lions. Hooper-Sharpe stopped and asked what I'd fired at. I told him and then pointed out the lions to him. By this time they'd got to rising ground and were clearly visible. I took another shot and off went the lions again.

I wasn't happy about leaving what I thought were injured lions and decided to cross the stream. Hooper-Sharpe backed me up with his shotgun. At the spot where the lions had been we found spots of blood. The vet reckoned it would be foolish to follow up as it was getting late and we agreed to move on. I was fed-up at losing my lion but we pushed on for a while before halting for the night. While the natives were setting up camp, Hooper-Sharpe cut up the pig and I took a rest, lying down with my head on my saddle. One of our natives disturbed my peace: '*Nangu lo ungulube*' (There's a pig). 'To hell with the pig,' I replied. 'Have a shot at it – it will be meat for the natives,' disagreed Hooper-Sharpe.

Grabbing my rifle I followed the native along a game trail. We neared a gully and the local stopped, pointing into it. There was a big tree on the bank and tiptoeing towards it, I looked into the gully. I could only see the hindquarters of the beast which appeared to be rolling in the sand. Raising my rifle I fired at what I could see. There was one hell of a roar. I didn't need to be told it was a lion! My heroic guide departed in haste with me in his wake – and I then stopped and went back. The lion was still roaring and trying to get up but its back was broken. I put it out of its misery with a second shot. Hooper-Sharpe came running up, showing off his veterinary skills by telling me I'd shot a lion! His assessment of the situation was, by his time, a little late! Our camp followers arrived and we climbed down into the gully to examine our prize. As we got alongside, it gave a deep groan to send us all either scrabbling up the bank or running down the gully. Hooper-Sharpe climbed a tree. But as there was no more movement from the lion, we covered our damaged pride to burst out laughing. It was too late to start skinning the lion so we tied it to a pole and hauled it out of the gully.

What a day! What a night! We hardly had a wink of sleep with lions roaring their displeasure all around the camp. Next morning Hooper-Sharpe took photos of me with the lion and at Matthysen's Farm we left the skin to be pegged out and dried. After the vet had completed his survey in the area, we continued on our way to the Falls. Only a day after we'd left Matthysens, Hooper-Sharpe was again up front when two big lions bounded across the road in front of him and into the long grass, beyond which there was a big burnt-out patch.

Hoping to get a shot – and not having learned my lesson – I dismounted and ran through the long grass to the cleared patch. I saw no sign of my quarry until I looked in the direction from which we'd come. The lions were bounding off, too far away for a shot. They could easily have been waiting for me in the long grass.

We arrived at the Falls and I was thankful to be home for a few days before returning to Matetsi. Later on the quarantine was lifted and what cattle had survived the lions and East Coast Fever were taken away. I returned to the Falls.

Captain St John had undertaken an inspection at the Falls and left for Bulawayo on the afternoon train. When it stopped at Kesi Siding, only about ten miles down the track, he got off and was walking up and down the siding when he noticed a nasty smell. From Matetsi he telephoned the stationmaster at Victoria Falls and asked him to pass on to us his instruction that we investigate. Henry Ford, whose first name was secretly Rufus, teamed up with the Permanent Way Inspector (PWI) and boarded the latter's trolley to arrive at the siding the following morning. They began a search and in the bush just off the track came on the body of a native. It was very obvious that he'd been murdered. Having noted the essential facts and burying the body, Henry and the railways inspector returned to the station. Evidence was soon forthcoming that the murdered native had slept in the police camp with another local a few days before the body was found. He was known to have had a fair sum of money on him when he left camp to return to his employer in Wankie.

Two days later I drew the short straw to go down to Kesi Siding with three native police and exhume the body. The Medical Officer from Wankie promised to arrive at dawn the next day to carry out the postmortem. It was not a pleasant job sleeping near the corpse or keeping fires going all night to repel wild animals. The doctor duly arrived and began his task. We smoked many cigarettes and drank much whisky to counteract the smell. We were very relieved to see the corpse reburied before travelling back to the station on the rail trolley. We obtained a description of the man seen in the company of the murdered man and I returned to the scene accompanied by a native constable. Then we went down the track towards Matetsi and at each ganger's cottage interviewed the locals for information regarding the movements of the wanted man. Soon I knew we were on the right track – literally – but it was a matter of moving quickly as our quarry was several days ahead of us. At Matetsi I asked Wankie to send a policeman to a particular village where I believed the suspect might be found. I also suggested that the village be approached when it was dark.

This was done but it seems the policeman cantered into the village making enough noise to raise the dead. The suspect was there but hearing the noise and correctly identifying the cause, he cleared off and was never captured.

Shortly after this I was sent to Bulawayo, remained there for about a month and was then sent to Gwanda. This was the district that provided conversations with many old prospectors and personally introduced me to small mines. As a result, I was to contract a bad case of gold fever! Gwanda was a large, pleasant and well-appointed camp. Some of the troopers stationed there in those days were later to become high-ranking police officers – the likes of Bridger (later a major), Onyett, Rochester and Fielding. From Gwanda I was transferred down to West Nicholson, a very busy mining centre with one sixty-stamp gold mine and numerous smaller operations.

One patrol took me across country towards Belingwe when we came on the spoor of a herd of sable antelope. A bit further on, to my left, I spotted a lion watching us over some long grass. I quickly dismounted but, by the time I'd taken aim, the lion had crouched down out of sight. Firing at the place where I expected him to be, out bounded the lion with a roar. He paused for a moment then tore off into the bush. We found a dead sable cow on which the lion had started to feed at that spot. My police boy and I followed the lion's trail, marked with drops of blood, but we had to abandon the pursuit. At the nearby village I advised the inhabitants that there was a wounded lion in the vicinity. A week or so later some of them turned up at the West Nicholson police camp saying they had found the remains of a lion. The only things worth keeping were some claws which they presented to me. Returning one day from a patrol near the Geelong Mine, I noticed a small quartz outcrop. I broke off several pieces and took them home. A few days later a miner, from whom I had borrowed pestle and mortar, watched me pan the quartz. We were both excited when gold showed in the pan but I sometimes wish those samples had been barren. They infected me with that incurable disease that was to stay with me for the rest of my life – gold fever.

It was not long after this when I decided to take my discharge from the Force. I reckoned it was time to go where:

There'll be no more evening stables,
No more morning drills,
No more attacks of fever
And no more quinine pills.
Of the Sergeant Major's anger
No more we'll bear the brunt.
There'll be no more canteen concerts
And no more kaffir beer.

# CHAPTER TEN

## Liebigs and Lions

In 1911, a company famous throughout the world for its 'bully beef' started ranching north of the Limpopo River, some sixty-five miles from my last station, West Nicholson. By then I had become the lessee of the West Nicholson Hotel and was offered and accepted the agency for the company, Liebig's. My role was to provide the transport Liebig's required to carry building materials to their ranch headquarters at Mazunga. A rough road had been constructed to Mazunga but beyond that there was nothing but wild bush country all the way to the Limpopo, the dividing line between the Transvaal and Southern Rhodesia. This part of the country was full of game and lions roamed the country unmolested.

Not being able to subcontract sufficient transport from others, I decided to invest in a wagon and a span of donkeys, which were very expensive in those days. Loading up the wagon, I sent it off on its first trip, carefully instructing the driver to have the donkeys kraaled at night. In the evening, three days after the wagon had left, I was socialising with some of my customers in the bar of the hotel. My African wagon driver appeared at the door and I knew at once that something had gone wrong. Before the man could speak, I told my customers that he was going to tell me that he'd lost some of my donkeys. He did. Lions had stampeded the donkeys out of the bush kraal at Mahado's Drift and four of them had been killed.

There was a veterinarian staying at the hotel who was going to Mazunga the following day. I decided to go with him. Before leaving, he suggested getting some strychnine to inject into the carcasses of the dead donkeys. I managed to do this. At Mahado's Drift we were told that there had been several lions. The dead donkeys, or what was left of them, were lying about in different parts of the veld. With the driver's help we were able to inject poison sufficient to kill anything that ate the donkeys. I asked the village chief to keep a sharp lookout for any lions found dead through eating the poisoned carcasses. A week or two later he reported back that he had found the remains of two lions, several jackals and other carnivores.

My next contract with Liebig's was to run a passenger and mail service from West Nicholson to Mazungu for which I purchased a buckboard and six mules. Before starting the service I had a proper stable built at Mahado's Drift, having no wish that the mules should meet the same fate as my donkeys. I went to Mazungu every fortnight and on an early visit the Liebig's manager, a Mr de Lassoe, said he would like to employ someone who would destroy lions on the ranch as a full-time occupation. Liebig's Ranch was losing too many cattle. I knew just the man – Yank Allen.

Yank stood well over six feet and, if I remember rightly, he came from Mexico. He feared no man and was not afraid to pick a quarrel. But if Yank took a liking to anyone, he was a friend for life. Kind hearted, he would give all he could to anyone needing help.

I'd first met Yank when I was in the Force. With a couple of others, he had been prospecting near the Farvie Mine, originally worked by the ancients, as had nearly all the mines in the Gwanda District. (Farvie Mine was owned by Lieutenant Herbert Henderson who in 1896 had won the Victoria Cross with Bulawayo Field Force during the Matabele Rebellion.)

One day Yank and his mates came upon a pile of rocks concealed in the undergrowth. Although it looked very artificial, one of the partners decided to pick it over. This exposed a lot of broken quartz which, when examined, was found to be full of visible gold. It seemed that the original miners in the dim and distant past had never got round to reaping their rewards. Yank and company put up their prospecting notice, then pegged off a block of territory. Wanting to make sure that the ground was registered as soon as possible, they decided to get to West Nicholson where the magistrate happened to be holding court. They borrowed a dilapidated cart from somewhere, a mule from another source and bits and pieces of harness, which had to be tied together with wire and string, from someone else. With this outfit they managed to reach West Nicholson.

The first place they made for was the village pub and after imbibing a few celebratory tots, they began boasting about their wonderful discovery. Another round or two of drinks and they got very talkative before going out to the cart and returning with a whisky case. Inside, wrapped up in paper, was one of the richest specimens of gold-bearing quartz I've ever seen. The sample was larger than a man's head. After more celebrating, Yank was dared to smash the rock to see if the gold went right through the quartz. He called for a hammer and broke up the specimen. The gold certainly ran right through the quartz. For days after I had my servants out in the veld looking for and finding small rocks showing gold and big enough to have mounted into tie-pins.

I've wandered somewhat from my tale but Yank Allen was the man I had to recruit as Liebig's Ranch official lion hunter. On my next trip to Mazungu, Yank Allen rode down with me, his pack of mongrel dogs following on by wagon in charge of his boy. On the way, Yank took a fancy to my rifle. He had a combination Martini/12 bore shotgun and we agreed on an exchange. I left Yank in the care of the manager who mentioned that he'd sent my wagon and driver off with a load of hides to West Nicholson earlier in the day and that he wanted me to have them railed out as soon as possible.

Leaving Mazungu early in the afternoon, we travelled on through the Jopempi Hills and were about six or seven miles from my stables at Mahado's Drift. I was relaxing in the back seat of the buckboard when my driver, a Dutchman, drew my attention to a hide lying in the road, which the mules shied at. I started to curse the native driver of my wagon for his carelessness. Going on a bit further, there was another hide abandoned in the dust. Then we saw the wagon in the distance and a few moments later its leading mules swerved across the road. Standing up in the buckboard, I saw a huge black-maned lion now loping towards us having been distracted from his interest in the wagon. I grabbed my newly acquired combination gun – loaded with both ball and shot – and fired both barrels, hitting him in the hindquarters. The beast roared angrily and appeared to sit down, growling and showing his teeth. I jumped off, shouting to the driver to hand me more ammunition from my belt in the front of the buckboard. The lion limped off into thick bush.

This must have been a relatively new experience for my very excited driver who was all for following the lion. I must admit that I wasn't so keen but we crept very cautiously into the bush, hearing him groaning and grunting ahead. We couldn't see him and, as the sun was down, I surrendered to discretion. The Dutchman was keen to continue, of course.

We continued our journey and coming up to the wagon I asked the driver what the hell he meant by losing hides. The poor devil explained to me that he had seen the lion following the wagon and that he and the leader had retreated to the top of the pile of hides. The leader had the bright idea of throwing a hide off the wagon, hoping the lion would stop and eat it. Leo was not at all tempted. So they decided to offer him another snack. Then they saw my buckboard approaching. The boss would make a much more savoury meal, they hoped!

Back at West Nicholson I discovered there were a couple of passengers for the return trip to Mazungu. I told them about the wounded lion and said that the driver would show them the spot. On their return they reported that the trees were full of vultures, either the lion was dying or dead. Having no rifle with them, they did not investigate further.

About this time I was offered a contract to cut a road from where the Beit Bridge now spans the Limpopo River. With Liebig's assistant manager, the late Captain Lane, and a gang of carriers, we travelled along native paths west of Mazungu until we struck the old Pioneer Road at Goongs Poort. It was then into the bush until we got to the Limpopo River where we decided on a spot that would make a fairly good crossing for animal transport – and named it Liebig's Drift. I had only a rough bearing to work on but I wanted to make the road as straight as possible. If anyone looks at the present map of that part of the county, I don't think the direction was too bad for the amateur I was.

Returning to Mazungu, I got together a gang of forty or fifty natives and found a white man to supervise the work. I returned with them to the Limpopo and remained there until the road was well underway and I was satisfied that the supervisor could carry on with the work. Before leaving I shot several large buck for the gang's consumption and arranged to return every fortnight to see how the work was going. Within a week I had to return to Mazungu to deliver several hundred pounds cash to pay Liebig's native labour. On the return journey, we found the going very slow. It had been raining and the road ran through black soil that meant heavy pulling for the mules. Nearing the Jopempi Hills, we saw a lot of guinea fowl and I shot several. That delayed us and it was getting dusk when we neared the place where I had encountered the previously mentioned black-maned lion.

The native driver reported that he had seen several big buck crossing the road up ahead. The mules, puffing and blowing, were going at a walk and at the place where the driver reckoned he'd seen the buck cross, I got down from the buckboard, taking my combination gun with me. Walking behind the buckboard, I kept a sharp lookout on the offside. Suddenly I saw a lion that was about to spring on the wheeler mule. I wasted no time firing the shot barrel full into its face. It roared and seemed to somersault. I didn't wait to see more but ran like hell, jumped into the buckboard and shouted to the driver to whip up the mules. 'There's another one,' he yelled back. But in all the excitement and not thinking, I had reloaded with the Number Four shot I'd used on the guinea fowl. I let drive at the second lion. A blind man couldn't have missed with shot ammunition but it was a different matter just how effective the volley was. The driver was convinced the lion was badly crippled and pulled the mules to a halt, thinking we were out of immediate danger.

Then he suggested going to look for the lion, asking me to let him have my revolver for his own peace of mind. We dismounted, inched into the bush and had only a few paces when he spotted the lion. It seemed as if it was dead but I wasn't so sure and told the driver that I'd have another shot at it. I did so. The lion sprang into the air and I wasn't far behind springing into the buckboard, yelling to the driver to do likewise. He still wanted to go back to where I'd fired at the first lion but I was taking no more risks that day.

By the time we arrived at my stables it was quite dark. During the night a Dutchman arrived with his wagon on the way to Mazungu. I told him about the lions. Feeling quite sure I had killed or badly wounded at least two, I asked him to search the bush when arriving at the place during the morning. Should he find the lions dead and if he would skin them for me, I would give him thirty shillings for each skin. A week later I saw him. He told me he had examined the place where I had wounded the lions and blood was all over the place – it looked as if I had wounded three. There had been four or five. He tried to get his boys to follow up the spoors with him but they refused. In the meantime, Yank Allen had heard about my adventures and had moved his camp accordingly. Two weeks later I arrived at Mazungu, who should be there but Yank Allen and this is how he greeted me: 'Well, a man that goes shooting goddamn lions with Number Four shot deserves to go plum hopping to hell!' It appears that Yank had followed up on the lions and caught up with three badly wounded ones which he'd finished off. On examining the skins he found them filled with Number Four shot holes, as Yank said 'like a goddamn pepper box.' However he scored in the end as he got paid, I think, five pounds for every lion he killed.

I continued on to the Limpopo River where my road gang was working. They had made fairly good progress but the trouble was water, having to send the donkey cart with drums several miles back for water at least two or three times a day.

I am not sure if it was on this occasion, but in the afternoon I had been out shooting and managed to shoot two Roan antelope. It was too late to return to camp for boys, so with the help of my gun carrier we covered up the buck with grass. Leaving camp early next morning, we heard the cry of a small buck in distress. I remarked to my gun carrier that I thought a leopard had caught a buck and he agreed with me. The noise came from a small kopje close by, so decided to climb it. On getting to the top, which was flat, imagine my surprise on seeing a lioness calmly walking across the small plateau with a small buck in its mouth, just like a cat with a rat. I stood amazed – until my native whispered, '*Du bula*' (Shoot). I hadn't got round to that as the 'cat-with-the-rat' spectacle was so amazing – and amusing.

I fired but my shot was low, hitting the ground just under the belly of the lioness. She then moved off, only a little more hurriedly. I reloaded, fired and missed again, hitting the ground this time just behind the lioness. She then disappeared down the far side of the kopje, still hanging on to the buck. The episode certainly didn't reflect well on my shooting ability that day!

# CHAPTER ELEVEN

## Prospects of Some Kinds

With the road to Mazungu completed, I was awarded a contract to carry mails and passengers from West Nicholson to Messina in the Transvaal. I bought a Cape cart and another buckboard and increased my mule numbers from six to eighteen. But the whole thing was doomed to failure. There were insufficient mails or passengers to make it pay and after running at a loss for three or four months, I decided to surrender the contract. In the meantime the West Nicholson mine had closed down which meant the hotel business was also losing.

I then started prospecting for gold in the vicinity of West Nicholson between the village and Jessie Mine. A small gully ran north to south close to the Granite Hills, about a mile west of the railway line. The rains had started so I thought I'd investigate this gully towards the mine. I had a native on each bank bringing a shovel of soil down to me in the gully itself. I found shed gold in almost every shovelful I panned.

I'd been doing this for several days when one night I had a vivid dream that I was pulling out pieces of gold from some clay. The next morning I continued prospecting up the gully. One sample contained a long and promising tail of gold. It was very exciting – perhaps my dream was an omen. There was an outcrop of schist close to where the promising sample of soil had been taken but by this time night was falling so I put off investigating until the next day. My patience went unrewarded – there wasn't a speck of gold to be found in the schist.

On the other side of the outcrop I took some more samples of soil and, on panning them, found more good tails of gold. Nearby was a slight rise leading up to an ironstone outcrop, so I continued taking samples and panning until the traces faded out. Going back to where I'd found my last good showing of gold, I marked out a six-foot by four-foot section and started the natives to digging a shaft. I don't know exactly why I decided on the shaft but after going down about three feet we hit a quartz leader. Sampling showed only about a two pennyweight panning so the gold I'd been getting in the soil hadn't come from that.

However, I persisted with the shaft. We were down about five feet and I'd 'knocked off' the natives for lunch when one of them – I remember he had five fingers and a thumb on each hand – came to where I was about to have scoff. He unwrapped a dirty piece of rag in his hand and emptied the contents on my table. More than a dozen pieces of pure gold winked back at me. 'Where in hell did you get this?' I exclaimed. '*Malinge lapa* (there's a lot there),' he answered, pointing to the shaft. I jumped up, ran like the devil to the shaft and jumped in. Looking at the walls, I couldn't miss the pieces of gold almost as big as my fingernail sticking out from what looked like seams of clay. Dancing with joy, I promised my natives goats, calves, chickens, anything I could think of. Then I started picking out the fragments of gold. Returning home that night, it gave my wife a great surprise when she saw all the gold in my can. Before the evening was out, I'd sold for a fair old sum a half-interest in the block of ground I'd pegged.

We registered the claim, calling it 'Bunny's Luck' for obvious reasons. Then we started developing the ground properly. When I'd sunk the shaft down some thirty feet, I put in a drive on the richest side of the shaft. At this stage an old police friend of mine visited the property. 'Snitch' Hutchings was a genuine Cockney. I invited him to go down the shaft with me and we climbed into the drive. Lighting a candle, I told Snitch to look up at the roof. 'Blimey, it looks just like a bleeding Piccadilly jeweller's shop,' he exclaimed.

Having mined about fifty tons of schist and clay, my partner and I decided to have a trial crushing. Hiring a five-stamp mill lying idle near the Farvie Mine and an experienced operator, we transported the ore in sacks from our claim. At the end of the crushing, the man who was doing the milling for us had to chisel the gold out of the box. After smelting, the bar of gold was taken to Bulawayo's Standard Bank and realized over eleven thousand pounds. Our sands in assay went fifteen pennyweights, which we sacked and took back to West Nicholson.

The next development was our purchase of a Tremain mill and several people from Bulawayo came to see our new equipment. I was offered several thousand pounds for my share but at that stage I wasn't interested. Later I did sell out to my partner for a few hundred pounds.

I then bought a half-interest in a gold property called Tuli Reef situated near the Tuli River, west of Gwanda. After we had developed this property further, we erected another Tremain mill. This time it was a failure: the stamps were too light for the class of ore and the values were none too high.

I'd volunteered for service at the start of the Great War but had been turned down because I was married with a family. I had another try and this time I was successful, joining up as a sergeant in the Southern Rhodesia Column, chasing Count Von Lettow in Tanganyika.

At the end of hostilities I returned to Rhodesia and got back to work on the Tuli Reef. Nearby I discovered another gold prospect which I named 'Freda' after my daughter. These two properties I sold to the well-known Bulawayo businessman, Jack Coghlan, whose brother's monument now stands in front of Town House.

Then it was time for a change from gold to diamonds. I decided to go down to the diggings at Bloemhof in the Union. There I found a partner and we did our own digging and 'rocking the baby'. When we reckoned we had sufficient ground ready for washing, we hired a man and his washing machine, agreeing to half-shares of any diamonds found. It was a complete blank. When it was time for the next wash, we decided to do our own sieving. An expert at the game can rotate the sieve of gravels in a butt of water and the diamonds are supposed to show themselves standing plumb in the centre on top of the gravels. My partner reckoned that he could do the trick – so I let him carry on. Need I record the complete absence of diamonds plumb in the centre – or anywhere for that matter?

The customary drill after a prospector had finished cleaning up for the day was to allow the 'Bantum' sorters – women and youngsters – to go over the gravels that had been washed, looking for any diamonds that had been overlooked. The morning after our last wash up, when the sorting had been done by my partner, we returned to our claim to be met with ridicule from a neighbour: 'You're a pair of bloody fools! The Bantum sorters went over your gravel and found a diamond.' Even if we had found the sorters, we had no claim to the diamond – such was the tradition.

Another day we witnessed a new rush underway with men running like hell all over the place and inviting us to join in. We pulled up our pegs and joined the scramble. Getting to the new ground, we hammered in our pegs like everyone else and then went back to the old claim to collect our picks and shovels. We found that our old site had already been re-pegged, shrugged it off and went on scratching at our new claim. The men around us 'found' in their first wash, we found nothing! But to cap the lot and turn the screw of futility, the claim we'd abandoned for the new ground turned out to be very rewarding for the new owner.

Despair and promise were all over the diggings. There was the case of the Dutch family, living on mealie meal while relying on other people to keep them in tea, coffee and so forth. They had a tumbledown light wagon with six donkeys. Their only child was very ill, mainly for want of proper food, and they decided to move off to another field not very far away. The day after relocating, the father and mother returned to their old claim for some reason or other. On looking at the ground they discovered a diamond which the rains had exposed. Their child died that day from starvation. The parents sold the diamond for over a thousand pounds a few hours later.

With similar tragic consequences, some of the diggers decided to play a trick on a Norwegian, a hard worker liked by everyone. One day after he'd left his claim to have lunch, these men got hold of the stopper of a decanter with the plug portion broken off. They half-buried this top portion with its facets showing in the bank of the river beside his claim. He was digging away during the afternoon when he noticed something shining amongst the gravels. Rushing over, he picked out the broken stopper. 'I have found, I have found!' he shouted, before running to his shack. When he discovered that he'd been made a fool of, he blew out his brains.

I was not sorry to leave the dark dramas of the diamond diggings when 1922's 'Rand Revolt' troubles erupted. I returned to Johannesburg, there to offer my services in the Special Police. The rioting was the consequence of the mine owners trying to cut the pay of white miners and give their jobs to natives. There were deaths and hundreds injured before the government managed to restore order. When the upheaval was over, I returned to Rhodesia and was engaged to go prospecting just east of Lusaka for a Northern Rhodesian company.

I travelled many hundreds of miles during my twenty-two months of prospecting off the beaten track in that very wild part of the country. Wild life of all sorts was to be seen in profusion and to add to the excitement Mazunga's lions had somehow sent a message north to their relatives that Bunny was on the menu! At one camp among the hills, my natives refused to stay if I remained there much longer. Every night it was either lions or leopards kicking up hell, especially if I had a lot of buck meat hanging in the trees. By day there was more variety of wild life and while panning in a small stream, I heard a crashing of trees, stamping of feet and natives yelling for my assistance. Looking downstream, I saw two of my natives going like blazes, being chased by a rhino. By the time I'd got my rifle from my tent, the rhino – and the natives – were lost in the hills. The natives returned to camp looking very much the worse for wear.

Moving my camp from the wilds, I arrived at a village where nearly all the occupants were suffering with conjunctivitis. Some years before, while travelling by train in the Congo, I'd met a South African who had suffered seriously with his eyes. He told me he had been cured with the Old Dutch remedy – Epsom Salts. As I had a fairly large supply with me, I set up practice, washing my patients' eyes with a solution of Epsom Salts. Doing this about three times a day left me little time for prospecting but within a week I had cured the lot – men, women and children – some of whom had been so blind they had to be led. They thought I was their saviour and of course passed on the good news to other villages. In no time native women and children from all over were being led and carried to my camp to be treated for the same complaint. Fortunately, I'd sent a runner back to headquarters for a further supply of Epsom Salts so I was able to continue the charitable work.

Some months later I was repaid for what I had done for the locals. I went down with dysentery and couldn't cure myself with what medicines I had. A native came to me and asked if I would drink some medicine he'd get from a certain tree. He guaranteed that it would cure my complaint. I was very weak, could hardly move and didn't care a damn what he gave me. Off he went into the bundu, returning about an hour later with some tree bark. He helped himself to my pestle and mortar and, placing some of the bark in the mortar, pounded it to a tobacco-like consistency. Then he boiled the concoction and gave me a cupful of the yellow and bitter liquid to drink After a few cupfuls of this, I felt much easier. Within twenty-four hours the dysentery had stopped and in two days I was completely cured. I offered this native a pound if he would show me the tree from which he'd got the bark. I wanted to send some to a doctor friend of mine for analysis. The native refused to let me on to his secret.

I discovered gold, both alluvial and reef, in many places. In the Luangwa valley I came on tough quartz boulders which had broken away from the mother lode, giving pan values of thirty pennyweights. The hills on the one side of the valley rose up to five hundred feet and, climbing to the top, I located the quartz reef. It seemed to be in place but, on trenching down a few feet, the reef was cut out. No doubt in the dim and distant past some movement of the earth had taken place in that part of the country, causing the reef to break away from the mother lode. Finding the real source would have required a lot of exploration and expensive development work. But I do know that at that time in the area there were numerous gold prospects very suitable for small worker development. But because different major companies held the concessions, no one was allowed to prospect until the concessions expired.

Game was everywhere in this part of the country. One day when out shooting for the pot, my native hunter spotted some Hartebeest. To me they seemed to be an unusually inquisitive kind of animal. When we got to within a hundred and fifty yards of them, I wanted to take a shot but my native stopped me and told me to get down low and he would entice the buck much closer to us. He did this just by bobbing up and down – the herd's leader would stop when he saw the native's head bob up but then come closer as he bobbed down. It was so amusing that I burst out laughing but I did manage to shoot one before they got away.

Another time we were at a place where there were lots of duiker. Going out with the same hunter, he took me to a place obviously frequented by the small buck. Plucking a leaf from a convenient bush, he tore off a piece, placed it in his mouth and started to make a noise like a small buck in distress. Duiker came running from all directions within minutes. I couldn't bring myself to shoot and was quite content to watch them looking for the one supposedly in distress. They were off like longdogs when they finally caught sight of us.

Trekking along with my team one day, we discovered what appeared to have been the home of a white man some time in the distant past. Only the buildings' foundations remained but there were old paths leading down to a beautiful stream supplied from the surrounding hills. I decided to camp and investigate further. Early next morning my natives, having gone to get water, came running back to report that about a dozen elephant were at the river. By the time I got down there, they'd moved off, no doubt having got wind of the intruders.

Looking about the riverbank, I noticed a banana plantation. There must have been nearly a thousand trees with huge bunches of bananas hanging from them. It was an open invitation but as soon as we got into the plantation to examine the fruit, first my natives started to scratch themselves and then I had to do likewise. Going in a little further, none of us could stand the irritation any longer. We ran like hell to the river, tore off our clothes and rubbed ourselves all over with sand, mud and any damn thing we could get hold of. It was no laughing matter – we scratched ourselves until we were almost raw.

It took a while to discover the cause of the trouble. Creepers had entwined themselves around the banana trees and on the creepers had grown a small velvety pod. Merely disturbing the pod released very fine threadlike particles. These particles, coming into contact with the skin, set up the irritation. The more one scratched, the worse it became. We couldn't risk putting on the same clothes until they were thoroughly washed, so we all walked back to camp as God made us – with the exception of myself. At least I had on a pair of boots, a helmet and carried my rifle! I would have given anything for a photo of our retreat from the river! There were no fig leaves about, otherwise we might have adorned ourselves appropriately.

The following day I sent my boss boy to the nearest village with instructions to return with the headman. On his arrival he told me that about fifteen years previously a white man had arrived from Broken Hill on a shooting trip and, taking a fancy to the spot, decided to settle down there. Later on I got the rest of the story from a government official. The new settler had applied for a land grant which was duly approved for only a nominal sum. It seems he was a remittance man, leaving home after having been accused of the apocryphal offence of striking the governess on the head with a roll of music. Banished to Rhodesia, he'd ended up at Broken Hill where he'd been employed as a secretary. But he found this too tedious so he threw away his pen, found this spot and settled down to grow bananas, pineapples and other fruits. Just when he started to reap the benefits of his work, he died of blackwater and was buried in this lonely spot by his natives. They had placed a cairn of rocks above his grave but the elephant had knocked it down. I felt obliged to rebuild the cairn.

Several lions seemed to be domiciled in the plantation. On a return visit, while I was in the midst of very carefully examining the pineapples with some of my team, two lions bounded across the path and into the plantation. I had no intention of going after them, bearing in mind my previous experience of the 'Itch'. But I will always remember that particular place as my Dream Farm.

Near my next camp on the top of a hill I discovered a body of schist containing large garnets. The surrounding country was rich with similar gems. I picked up one in particular which was as large as my fist, took it back to Bulawayo and handed it over to the museum. Some years later I visited the museum expecting to see my garnet on exhibit. It was missing and on making enquiries no trace of it could be found.

It was time for me to get back to Bulawayo, there to await the return of my chief and report to him. In the meantime he had obtained a concession near the Sanyati River, about ninety miles northwest of Sinoia. Before my boss arrived, I saw in the newspaper that George Lamby and five or six natives had been in a punt crossing the Sanyati River. The frail craft had capsized midstream, throwing the occupants into the river where they'd been taken by crocodiles. George Lamby, a fine man, had visited my camp in the Luangwa Valley, Northern Rhodesia. Dozens of natives had been employed to search the riverbanks, reported the newspaper, but no trace of any of the party had been found. A day or so later my chief arrived, looking very down in the mouth. He'd been present when the accident happened. He told me he'd been standing on the south bank with a couple of company directors who were on their way to the Copper Queen Mine, five miles on the other side of the river. With the river in flood, they dismissed any attempt to cross that day in the flimsy punt. Lamby insisted it would be quite safe and, to prove it, decided to cross over with some boys. In midstream a strong current of water hit the punt and capsized it. Lamby was last seen swimming strongly for the bank when he suddenly raised his hands in the air and disappeared, no doubt pulled under by a crocodile.

A monument to George Lamby was erected on the north bank but is seldom seen by Europeans. That part of the country has become desolate since the closing-down of Copper Queen. A few days later my duties took me to the scene of the accident but I had no difficulty crossing since the river was low.

I spent eighteen months prospecting this particular part of Southern Rhodesia and discovered gold, galena (lead), copper and zinc. I'm assured that in time to come this will be a big mining centre. It only requires capital and people with guts who are not afraid of tsetse fly and can do without the cinema every night. There's game of all kinds, wonderful fishing and stretches of water on the Sanyati River where one can canoe to one's heart's content. What more is there to be asked for in this life?

In these days of motor transport, with all the old roads fixed up, one can leave the Copper Queen at noon and arrive in Salisbury, approximately one hundred and sixty miles away, in time for dinner. From another aspect, it is terrible to think of the thousands of buck that have and are being slaughtered in this region because of the tsetse fly. All the hides, horns and hooves wasted – when surely some use could be made of them.

# CHAPTER TWELVE

## Barotseland, then Home

After prospecting in this area of Mashonaland for eighteen months, I was asked to go to Barotseland to look at a concession granted to the company by Paramount Chief Yeta. My orders were to proceed to Lusaka in Northern Rhodesia where I was to be joined by two other men. We were to be taken by lorry up to the Kafue River where each of us was to await a team of carriers being recruited by Yeta's son. I was the last to leave, having to wait longer for my team. It was about a hundred miles to the concession at the junction of the Dongwe and Lalafuta rivers.

I was supplied with a bicycle of all things but it did have the advantage of acting as a traverse wheel to enable me to check distances when plotting. However the country was covered with small ant heaps so it was impossible to ride very far. There was game everywhere and a common sight was the sight of hartebeeste and wildebeeste grazing next to each other. Once again, the hartebeeste showed the curiosity I'd experienced before. They would gallop along, then all line up in a row – like soldiers on parade – right across my path as if to challenge my right of way. When I got close to them I would ring my bicycle bell, they would 'about turn' and off they'd go to parade again further on.

At last I arrived at the place designated to be our headquarters, only to find that one of the men who had preceded me was down with fever. I advised him to return, procured fresh carriers and sent him off in a machila with instructions to the head boy to hurry with him to the Kafue. I sent another runner to the mine at Matala Hill requesting that a lorry be sent to the Kafue River to meet the sick man so that he could be taken to the hospital in Lusaka.

Copper was the mineral we were looking for and although dozens of places showed the typical green copper stain, none turned out to indicate any real promise. Our camp was on the side of a long valley, about a quarter of a mile wide, with thick bush on either side. In the early morning or at sunset, one had only to look up or down the valley to see eland, sable, roan, hartebeest and quagga. There was no need to go far when meat was required. There were also packs of hyenas that came howling around the camp at night.

On one occasion my cook had left a saucepan containing some stew on a box in my dining room – just a temporary shack made of poles and grass. During the night I was awakened by a crash in the dining room. Next morning, on investigating the cause, we found that animals, almost certainly hyena, had bitten clean through the aluminium saucepan.

The following night I fixed up a trap gun in the dining room. A piece of meat was tied on to the end of the barrel and a string connected the trigger and table leg. About midnight the gun went off and there was a scampering of animal feet. Going out with my shotgun to see what had happened, I found teeth, blood and what looked like bits of jaw but no sign of the wounded animal. In the morning I sent natives to follow up the spoor and they found a dead hyena. Its jaw had been blown to pieces. After what had happened to the saucepan, I examined the gun barrel carefully just in case those very powerful jaws had also damaged the gun.

Another night wild dogs could be heard killing a small buck just on the edge of the compound. Calling the natives to bring grass torches and their assegais, we went towards the commotion. The natives were somewhat lacking in bravery so I decided to play a trick on them. Stamping my feet, I pretended to run back, as if something was after me. The natives turned and went like hell, with cries as they passed of '*Maiwe! Maiwe!*' They were on top of each other to such an extent that their assegais were prodding the bare behinds of the ones in front. I couldn't sleep the rest of the night for laughing. One day we were traversing a part of the country with one native in front carrying marker flags, then me about thirty yards behind and then a second native pushing my bicycle. My rifle was being carried by a third native behind the one with the bicycle. The flag bearer had just passed a big tree some twenty yards away on his right and, as the native with the bicycle and I were passing, a roar went up. From behind the tree sprang a lion. The beast looked left then right. I shouted for the gun bearer to bring the rifle but, like the rest of us, he was frozen to the spot. The lion, which had a full-grown mane, bounded off in the direction from whence it had come. Life came back to me. I ran to the paralysed gun bearer, grabbed the rifle and made after the beast with two natives in close support. Getting to an open vlei, we saw him crossing over to the other side before he stopped and stood by an ant heap. Kneeling, I took aim and pulled the trigger. There was only a click – the cartridge was a dud. Reloading, I fired and there was no mistake this time. The lion sprang into the bush after he was hit. At the ant heap, we found blood, which we followed up until it went into very thick bush. Back at my camp, natives from the village arrived in no time with chickens as a gift for the Bwana who had met the big bad lion face to face and – according to them – destroyed it.

I was very thankful when orders came for the party to return to Lusaka. Getting together about a hundred carriers, we trekked back to civilization after being out in the blue for twenty months.

Severing my connection with the one company, I went to Ndola to undertake contracts for another exploration outfit. One assignment, given to me by the well-known Copperbelt geologist, Dr J.A. Bancroft, was to do the pitting* at Mindola, now one of biggest and busiest places after Nkana.

(* 'Pitting' in this context is believed to be the sinking of a series of shafts or 'pits' in the vicinity of an outcrop to confirm the presence of an ore-bearing seam. *Editor*.)

Then the Great Depression came and all contracts stopped. I decided to return to Southern Rhodesia and peg my gold prospects near the Copper Queen.

I teamed up with Jimmie, an old acquaintance, and leaving Northern Rhodesia in a Ford vanette, we drove to Kafue on the main road to Southern Rhodesia. From there we made for the Zambezi River where the Chirundu Bridge now spans it. The road was only a bush track but my partner was a careful driver and we took our time. An amusing incident happened to us soon after we had been told about the Salvation Army Mission we would pass on the northern side of the Zambezi. We were about five miles away when we met a native on a bicycle in full Salvation Army uniform, complete with cap. He asked us if we had seen another car on our way. The Mission was anticipating an inspection by the Army's Colonel Moffat. We told him we had met no one, he continued on his way and we on ours. On approaching the Mission, we sounded our hooter.

Nearing the first house, we saw a man running out and putting on his jacket before he disappeared around the other side of the house. Suddenly a band started – I've forgotten the tune but I think it was 'See the Conquering Hero Comes'. The man in the jacket reappeared, all smiles until he saw us. His expression changed to one of disgust. Turning on his heels, he went away and stopped the band. Coming back, he explained rather ungraciously that on hearing the hooter he had mistaken us for Colonel Moffat.

We asked the missionary if there was somewhere we could stay for the night but his attitude indicated that he didn't want us around. He advised us to go on about six miles where we would find a stream and camp there. This we did and while Jimmie was cooking our meal we heard a car at the stream. It seemed to be having trouble climbing the bank. We concluded that it was the overdue Colonel who had come the other way.

The following morning we arrived at the Zambezi River where we were forced to remain for a day until 'Jimmie the Greek' (not my companion) agreed to embark our car onto his homemade punt and ferry us across to Chirundu on the far bank.

Safely across and back in Southern Rhodesia, we found that driving the old Ford up the escarpment was no easy task but we just managed it and two days later reached Sinoia. From there we continued down to the Sanyati River, which we managed to cross after cutting and laying branches over the sandy parts, and arrived at the old Emerald Mine where I'd prospected a few years earlier. All this area was now open for reallocation and we started pegging the following day.

The heavy rains had started and very soon flooded rivers cut us off. Undeterred by the weather, we started to sink a shaft on one of my old discoveries after Jimmie had managed to recruit some natives from a nearby village. I carried on prospecting. Game was very plentiful. Jimmie hadn't done any game hunting and decided to try his hand one afternoon. Taking a native with him, he made towards the river. He returned at about six o'clock, very excited. He'd seen several big buck standing at the edge of the river on the far bank. He'd fired and killed three, so he claimed. I was a bit fed up at this waste of ammunition. Furthermore, the buck were on the other side of the river and I asked Jimmie what plans he had to retrieve them with the river running so high. No trouble, he'd cross early next morning at the drift.

Taking the vanette with about six natives on board, he left as planned and at the drift they all stripped. Forming a chain gang, they started to wade across with the water almost up to their armpits, the last native holding Jimmie's rifle well above his head. Fortunately there were no crocodiles evident and after a bit of a struggle they got over. Now they had to walk two miles up the riverbank to the spot where the buck had been downed. Nearing their objective, their surprise on seeing two crocodiles pulling one buck into the river can be imagined. Another was left with its leg already torn away.

Close by was a fourteen-foot python, coiled as if it was asleep and with the middle part of its body noticeably swollen. Jimmie fired, killed it and, wanting the skin as a trophy, got the natives to skin it. Opening up the stomach they found a full-grown rabbit which the snake could only have swallowed an hour or so previously. When the team returned to camp, I was presented with the rabbit. I had it skinned and made into an appetising stew which Jimmie and I consumed – totally ignoring the venison he'd rescued at the cost of much energy from the crocodiles!

After developing two or three shafts, we disposed of our interests in the claims and Jimmie and I returned to Salisbury. Some time later I heard the sad news that he had been killed on a mine near Penhalonga. A native dropped a drill down the shaft at the bottom of which Jimmie was working.

May his soul rest in Peace.

Time marched on and I returned with my wife to the Umfuli looking for alluvial gold in the river. Our camp consisted of a large tarpaulin stretched over poles with grass on top, our kitchen was the open veld with nails driven into a tree to hang the pots and pans on and act as our dresser. The local menfolk in this part of the country seemed to be a lazy and lousy lot and didn't want work. I persuaded some of their women to take on the pick and shovel work. Although there were some with children strapped on their backs and others with toddlers clinging to their skirts, they worked like Trojans – or should that be Amazons.

Lions roared every night – they'd obviously heard I'd arrived in their part of the world – and we lost one of our dogs to a leopard. Early one morning we heard shots and put it down to natives shooting game. About an hour later two natives arrived in camp carrying meat, as we thought. My wife was making out a list of foodstuffs she required from Sinoia. Seeing the natives, she remarked that there would be no need now for the errand boy to bring back meat from town. The natives approached us with broad grins on their faces and we saw they were carrying the skin of a lioness with the head still attached and eyes wide open. I swear one eye winked at my wife, twitching caused by the nerves, I supposed. As my wife was very fond of brains, I suggested we should get the lion's extracted for our lunch. She was not amused but I managed to duck just in time! The natives said they'd encountered the lioness with two cubs. Suddenly the mother had charged, both natives had fired and dropped her. The cubs ran into the reeds on the riverbank.

Not long after this a native came to report that a lion had taken a man from a nearby village. The victim had two wives who lived in different huts. He had been to see one wife to tuck her up for the night and, his duty done and returning to the other, the lion sprang on him and killed him on the spot. The two wives and children could hear his screams but could do nothing to help. A search party followed up the spoor the following morning but all they found were the man's feet.

Hearing there was the real possibility of war with Germany, my wife and I packed up our traps and returned to Salisbury.

War was declared and once again I found myself clad in the King's uniform as Regimental Sergeant Major of the Internment Camp Guard in Salisbury. And this is where I must take leave of my 'Incidents', longing for the day when peace is restored and I can return to the wide blue yonder and lead the only kind of life worth living:

*'When gold and silver becks me to come on.'*

*Kahlulu (The Rabbit)*

# THE WANDERERS

**A story by W.H. Rabbetts published in the January 1961 issue of the *OUTPOST*, the magazine of the British South Africa Police**

*My Old Man's a Fireman*
*Watcher think of That*
*He wears Gaw Blimey Trousers*
*And a little Gaw Blimey Hat*
*He wears a Blooming Choker*
*Around his Blooming Froat;*
*My Old Man's a Fireman*
*On a Donald Currie Boat.*

I heard this refrain being sung about ten o'clock on a very wet evening as I was walking along the Dock Road, Cape Town, many years ago. I recognised the voice. It was an old shipmate I had last seen somewhere in South America. I hurried after the singer. When near him I shouted, 'Hullo, Tich, what in hell are you doing in this part of the world?' He stopped and, on recognising me, almost crushed my ribs with the hug he gave me. 'Bill, old boy,' he said, 'I lost my last ship, the *Scot,* having got soused on tickey beer and overslept myself on the beach when she sailed. I now find myself, as usual, broke and on the rocks. What about a beer?'

I told him I was almost in the same boat as he, but half of what I had was his, just as we shared in the old days. So to celebrate our meeting we proceeded to the old 'Silver Tree,' where we imbibed tickey beer. At closing time we began to think of a bed, so decided, instead of the beach, to go to the Salvation Army Home, where a bed would cost us sixpence each and sixpence for two 'doorsteps' of thick bread and butter with a cup of tea each in the morning. The following day we heard they wanted some stewards on the railway dining cars running between Cape Town and

Johannesburg, so we decided to chance our arm. Tich had been a stoker on the ships, so one can imagine how he would shape as a steward. We presented ourselves at the Catering Department where, after a lot of questioning, the manager decided to give us a trial, provided we procured – at our expense – some white suits.

This we did by exchanging a suit of my clothes at a second-hand clothes shop. We reported for duty that evening in time to join the train leaving for Johannesburg at nine o'clock. There were two other stewards on the train and we explained to them that we knew very little about the job, so would they play the game and help us through? This they promised to do. The following morning at breakfast, Tich and I were given two or three tables to look after.

The train was going at a good speed and rocking quite a bit. There was an elderly man, his wife and a nice-looking daughter who came and sat at one of Tich's tables. As they were seating themselves, Tich kept winking at me and casting his eyes at the girl. When they had seated themselves, Tich went up to them and said to the father, 'It's a bit rough this morning, Governor.' The old man cast a wicked look at Tich and barked, 'Where's the menu?' 'The what?' asked Tich. With that, one of the other stewards placed the menu into Tich's hand. He looked at it and said, 'Oh, the card that you want to feed your face on!'

With that, up went a laugh from all the other diners in the saloon, including the daughter of the old gent; her laughter was more hilarious than the rest. They then gave Tich their order. The old man and his wife wanted porridge, whilst the girl wanted poached eggs. Away went Tich for the order. Returning with it, he put the porridge down in front of the old man. Just then the train gave an extra lurch. Off shot the eggs, right into the old man's porridge. 'Blimey,' said Tich, 'it's like being on the ocean wave.' Another roar of laughter went up.

Tich tried to apologise, but the girl told him not to worry, as they were her eggs which had made the slip and she was sure her 'dear daddy' was not cross; he could get another plate of porridge and she more eggs, but that he (Tich) had better carry one plate at a time, as she could see that he was not used to that job. Tich said, 'Thank you, my dear,' and then, 'I beg your pardon; I forgot myself.' The old gent said, 'Don't forget again.' 'No, my dear, I mean no, sir!' replied Tich.

After breakfast was finished, Tich was told by the head steward that if he did not do better he would have to 'get out.' Lunch went off fairly well but the passengers in the saloon were hoping for something to happen which would liven things up a bit. At sundown Tich was serving drinks in the saloon and was invited to have a quick one, which he did on several – too many – occasions. At dinner time he felt quite merry, but carried out his duties fairly well. The good-looking daughter was watching him with a smile on her face, hoping, I think, that he would say or do something foolish that would start them all laughing.

The old man ordered a small bottle of 'fizz.' Now Tich did not know the first thing about opening a bottle of champagne, although he was quite good at opening bottles of tickey beer! He was instructed by the head steward how to take off the wire and gently release the cork. He took the wire off all right, but didn't hold the cork. Out it popped, hitting the old gent on the head. The cork was closely followed up by a stream of champagne. The daughter screamed with laughter and so did the others in the saloon.

This was too much for the old father, who raved and demanded the head steward to take Tich away before he threw him off the train himself. When asked by the head steward where he had been a waiter, Tich replied, 'The only waiting I've done has been for the pubs to open. My job is a stoker, feeding coals into a firebox, not food into people's mouths. I'll get off at the next station.'

He went along to the compartment where we had our few belongings. I followed him. 'Bill,' he said to me, 'this is no job for me; let's get off at the next stop and get a job on some farm for a change.' I agreed to this. Arriving at a place called Brandfort, we left the train. We asked the stationmaster where the nearest farm was and if there were any jobs going. He told us that a sheep farmer named Giles, about ten miles away, was looking for men to help with the shearing. He gave us directions but as it was late he allowed us to sleep in the waiting room.

Starting off early next day, we made for the sheep farm. Tich said, 'What the hell do we know about a sheep, let alone cutting his wool off? If we could only see it being done for a little while we could take a chance.'

I told Tich that there was no way that I was going to attempt the job of shearing sheep, even if we were offered it. 'Right,' said Tich, 'I will, and when I've learned the game I'll teach you.'

Arriving at the farm, we were met by the farmer who kindly asked us to have something to eat and drink. When finished, he asked us where we were making for. When we said we were looking for work, he offered us a temporary job to assist with the shearing. I kept quiet, but Tich said, 'I have not done much shearing in my time, but no doubt I'll soon pick it up again.'

The farmer invited us to the shearing pens, where the work was in progress and was being done by natives. After a little while Tich decided he'd have a go. The farmer gave him a pair of shears and Tich went to where the sheep were penned, waiting their turn to be sheared. Getting hold of a ram, he dragged it from the pen to where the others were shearing. After a struggle he got the sheep on its back, with its head between his legs. Taking the shears, he started to shear the fleece down the centre of its stomach towards its hind legs. When nearing the hind legs he must have nipped him. There was a loud baa-baa! The ram twisted itself loose, upsetting Tich in the process. As he was getting back on his feet, the ram butted him in the behind and then chased him. Tich ran like blazes and climbed up on to the fence – with the ram standing on its hind legs trying to get at him. 'To hell with sheep farming, Bill,' he shouted, 'let's go diamond digging.' Waving farewell to the farmer, we moved on again.

Towards sundown we arrived at another farmhouse. Cattle were in the yard and cows were being milked. The farmer's wife saw us approaching. When we got to her, she complained that her husband was away and that some of the natives had not turned up for the milking. Would we be good enough to help her by milking some of the cows? Tich volunteered at once. The farmer's wife gave us a bucket and a milking stool each and told us to take any cow, as they were all quiet. Now as a boy I had lived with an uncle who was farming in Dorset and I'd been taught to milk cows. But Tich confessed that he'd only seen cattle when they were hung up in a butcher's shop.

Off we started. I picked out a cow and sat down to do the necessary. Suddenly I heard a plaintive moo, the clash of a bucket and the sound of running feet. Looking up, I saw Tich running for dear life to the fence. He had made another mistake. He remained on the fence until the milking was over and the cattle had been driven out to graze. The farmer's wife asked Tich what had happened. He replied that when he tried to milk the cow it turned its head and looked at him with such a wicked look that he'd got the wind up and had run for his life.

However, we were invited to stay the night. The farmer returned later in the evening and, producing a bottle of brandy, he invited us to a drink. After a couple of tots, Tich started to sing some old sea shanties, much to the delight of the farmer and his wife. The following morning we decided to work our way to the coast. A farmer's life was not suitable for either of us.

Arriving at a small town, we found ourselves broke. It was then Tich suggested that we could make a few shillings 'busking' – that is, singing songs in a bar. We approached the barman at one hotel, explained that we were broke and that we hoped to make a few shillings by singing a couple of songs in the public bar. He was very sympathetic and asked the men in the bar if they would mind. They were agreeable. Tich started off with 'Way Down Upon the Swanee River.'

Almost at once came the response: 'Blimey, can't you give us something new?'

'Rightho,' said Tich. He then started the old song, 'I'm Only a Bird in a Gilded Cage.'

'Hell,' came the same voice, 'what are you – a blooming nightingale? Give your pal a chance.'

'Very good,' said Tich obediently.

So I started: 'I am but a Poor Blind Boy.'

'Blind drunk,' someone shouted. 'For God's sake, give them a couple of bob and let them go somewhere else.'

This they did, with a parting remark not to spend it all on beer.

We did two more bars, collecting a few shillings, sufficient to pay for a meal each and a beer or two. We then moved on to the next town where there was a circus. Thinking there might be a job at the circus, we approached the manager – or manageress, as she was.

She was a dear kind soul but, when we approached her, she wanted to know what the hell we wanted. When we told her, she replied that she wanted no bloody stiffs around her show. As we were moving off, she had second thoughts and called us back. She wanted a man to enter the lion's den with the lion-tamer and be shaved by a second man. If we cared to take the job on, it was ours. When we asked her to give us time to talk it over, she replied: 'Hell, do you think my lions would eat things like you?'

Tich and I went to one side to discuss the offer. 'Crikey,' he said, 'This is the end of everything, Bill. It's bad enough shovelling coals into a furnace on board a ship, but to be shaved in a lion's den makes me want to be sick. If we take this job on and anything happens to me, will you promise to write to my poor old mother and tell her how I died?'

Despite Tich's pessimism, we decided to take the job on if the pay was worth it. We went back and told the lady we'd take the job on, depending on how much we would be paid. Satisfied with what she promised, we were instructed to bring a razor, brush, soap and towel and to be seated in the front row for the performance. When our time came, we would be announced and were to walk across the arena to the lions' den and enter it when the trainer opened the door of the cage. One of us had to sit on a chair, have the towel placed around his neck and be shaved whilst the trainer was putting the lions through their performance. Tich decided that he would be the one to be shaved…by me!

At nine o' clock that night we were sitting with the crowd when it was announced that two 'gentlemen' would enter the lions' den, where one would shave the other. Cheers went up, but Tich's heart and mine started to do a gallop. As we walked across the arena to the cage, Tich whispered, 'My God, something has gone wrong with me innards.'

'Me too,' I replied, 'but we can't turn back now.'

Getting to the steps of the cage, Tich was handed the chair that we had to take inside. Said Tich, 'I can hardly carry myself in, let alone a chair.'

Just then the trainer, who'd been conducting the lions through their tricks, got to the gate. Pulling back the bolt, he opened the gate slightly and told us to get in quick. We did so but no sooner had we put a foot inside the cage, the lions gave one hell of a roar. Tich and I turned as one man for the gate. But it was too late – we were locked in.

The audience roared with laughter when they saw us turn for the gate, probably thinking it was part of the act. Placing the chair in position, Tich sat down, but he was shaking so much – certainly not part of the act – that the flimsy chair threatened to give way beneath him. I wrapped the towel around Tich's neck and started to rub the soap over his cheeks. Then I began with the brush, with one eye on the lions, and somehow managed to get soap in his mouth, nose and eyes. I then started with the razor, but I was so shaky I almost cut off his nose. The trainer did something to the lions that made them roar again. Up jumped Tich and made for the gate, myself after him. The audience simply screamed with laughter, but for us it was no laughing matter.

The trainer must have realised that things had gone beyond a joke. Keeping the lions at the one end of the cage, he worked his way back to the gate, pulled the bolt, and let us out. The cheers that went up did not concern us. We were out of that cage and only wanted to collect our money and get as far away as possible from those lions and the town itself. We certainly had no intention of entering that cage again for double or even treble the amount paid us.

Leaving town the following day, we managed to jump a goods train proceeding towards Durban. Unfortunately we were spotted when nearing a siding, so had to get off in a hurry. Getting to the main road, we were able to hitch several lifts on the way to Durban where we arrived at last, very thankful to see the ocean once again. There were several ships in the docks so we decided to do the rounds on the off chance of getting a job. The first one we boarded, a mail boat, was short of men so we both signed on, Tich as a stoker, myself as a deck hand. In two days we were well out to sea. On the third day, imagine my surprise when, scrubbing down the decks, I looked up to see the old gentleman with his wife and pretty daughter, our passengers on the train on which we'd been as stewards.